Unless otherwise indic
from the King James Version of the Holy Bible. Other
translations may include the New American Standard Bible
(NASB), the English Standard Version (ESV), the New
Living Translation (NLT), and the Amplified Bible (AMP).
Any words bolded within the Scriptures are emphasis
added by this author. References to "Strong's" refer to
Strong's Exhaustive Concordance.

TO TITHE OR NOT TO TITHE? THAT IS THE QUESTION

For other spiritual resources, contact:

ChristLife, Inc.
PO Box 1033
Niagara Falls, NY 14304

(716) 622-7320

Visit our web site: www.Christ-like.net
Email: christlife@christ-like.net

Printed in the United States of America

Published April 2020 by ChristLife, Inc.

Author:
Dallmann, Robert, 1962–

Acknowledgments

To begin with, I want to honor God the Father, Who has given me all things that pertain to life and godliness. Anything that any of us has to offer has been given to us by God.

Above all, thanks to Jesus Christ for drawing me to Himself and saving me from my sins. Without His death, burial, and resurrection, I would have no interest in understanding the things of God.

I gladly acknowledge the Holy Spirit, Who leads and empowers me.

I am also very grateful to God for my family, for my wife and three sons. The Lord has blessed me with them and I love and appreciate them.

P.T. Harvey is also owed a debt of thanks for her efforts in editing this book. She has been a faithful encourager of the **ChristLife, Inc.** ministry.

She is an author herself having written several books for a community organization in the past, a Christian newsletter for eleven years, and varied other writings, including prophetic poetry. She has authored Scout – A Journey in Faith, a book about her life's journey of faith, sharing some of the wondrous things God has done.

Robert Dallmann

Preface

And now onto the topic at hand:

Tithing today is a complicated subject to discuss. Have you ever discussed tithing with anyone who holds the opposite conviction as you? If so, you can likely testify that the discussion was intense.

In this book, we will review the biblical principles of giving and examine New Testament patterns of generosity. The proposal is that, as Christians, we follow the model outlined in the New Testament.

The premise of this book is simple; a person led by the Holy Spirit will never be directed to greediness but rather to generosity. Such a person will always seek to exceed the minimum standards of the Law.

> *"Do we then make void the law through faith? God forbid: yea, we establish the law."* (Romans 3:31)

The prayerful hope for this book is that we will be led to:

…a greater trust in Jesus,
…a far more thankful heart for His salvation,
…an increased depth of relationship with God,
…a "double honor" appreciation for His faithful servants,
…a far more generous spirit,
…increased provisions for evangelism and discipleship,
…increased freedom from the bondage to money,
…and more.

Table of Contents

Chapter 1 - Introduction

Our prayer is that this writing will help to clarify why and how we are to give. Biblical giving is an expectation of God and serves His Kingdom in many ways.

Faithful biblical giving is Holy Spirit-led, cheerful, and patterned after New Testament examples. Honest biblical giving never seeks to put believers in bondage to tithing, nor will it ever cause anyone to violate God's Word.

Obedience cannot earn God's grace! But it is rewarded by His blessing.

Disobedience can earn God's disapproval!

While Legalists obey God's Law to earn something, Lovers of God obey God because they love God the Father, Jesus the Son, and the Holy Spirit!

While legalists try to earn salvation, prestige, and honor, greater rewards in Heaven, or to meet some other goal through obeying God's Law, Lovers of God follow Him because they can! The Holy Spirit leads them to live God-honoring lives and empowers them to do so.

Biblical Observation:

New Testament Christians gave **far more** than tithes!

Modern Christians give **far less** than tithes! And the world suffers because of that.

Chapter 2 - Give As The Holy Spirit Leads You!

The premise of this book is that Christians should give as led by the Holy Spirit.

Many who oppose the idea of "tithes," will point out that we should give as the Holy Spirit leads us.

Spirit-led giving is a wonderful belief that we should all put into practice! If all or even most Christians were indeed led by the Holy Spirit regarding their giving, no truly God-birthed ministry would lack funding. None of God's anointed servants would need to oversee extensive fund-raising campaigns. They would be able to spend their time devoted to prayer and their ministry in the Word of God.

> *"But we will give ourselves continually to prayer, and to the ministry of the word."* (Acts 6:4)

Matthew Henry's Whole Bible Commentary makes the following observation:

> "...The first contention in the Christian church was about a money-matter..." (Refer to Acts 6:1, where the "Grecians" murmured against the "Hebrews" regarding an alleged neglect in regards to the dispensing of charity.)"

Matthew Henry goes on to note that large amounts of money were received for the relief of the poor and that a dispute arose over the inequitable distribution of this charity. See Acts chapter 4 and 5 for examples of the money donated to the new Christian leadership, including the story of Ananias and Sapphira's gift.

2

It is interesting to note that the **first issue of contention** in the Christian church remains a huge issue today, **MONEY**!

If you do not think that monetary giving amongst Christians today is a big deal, please join a Christian discussion group on-line and bring up the topic. It will not take long for you to learn how much of an issue money really is. Suggestion: For the most impact, join a large on-line Christian discussion group and begin a dialogue about tithing, and discover what will happen.

In contrast, *"Give as the Holy Spirit Leads You!"* is the premise of this entire book. Typically, when this statement is made, there often seems to be an underlying thought that the Holy Spirit may lead you to give less than the Law required.

Some questions that come to mind when meditating on this notion may be:

* Are there any examples in the Bible when the Holy Spirit led someone not to **tithe**?

* Does the Bible ever speak disparagingly about tithing?

* Are there any examples in the Bible of the Holy Spirit leading anyone to **violate the Law** of God? Or to do **LESS** than the Law required?

If the examples from the Bible are studied carefully, one might be surprised at what the Holy Spirit will lead us to do. Since the Holy Spirit Himself empowers and enables us, it is unlikely that we will ever be led to do less than the Law (which He wrote) requires.

Let's a look at what the Bible says concerning these questions.

Are there any examples in the Bible when the Holy Spirit led someone not to tithe?

Initially, this could seem like a challenging question to answer. However, if you read what is said about money and giving in the New Testament, you will find that nobody who is being led by the Holy Spirit ever gave less than the tithe required by the Law. For example:

The Widow's Mites

> *"And Jesus sat over against the treasury, and beheld how the people cast money into the treasury: and many that were rich cast in much. (42) And there came a certain **poor widow**, and she threw in **two mites**, which make a farthing. (43) And **he called unto him his disciples**, and saith unto them, Verily I say unto you, That this **poor widow hath cast more in**, than all they which have cast into the treasury: (44) For all they did cast in of their abundance; but she of her want did **cast in all that she had, even all her living**."* (Mark 12:41-44)

When giving is discussed in Christian circles, it is not uncommon to hear the idea that those who have nothing should give nothing and that those who have much should give more. While there is Scripture that seems to suggest such thinking (e.g., Luke 12:48 unto whom much is given, much is required), is this the type of thinking that impressed Jesus?

Please notice the **bolded phrases** in the widow's mite story above and take note of the details.

4

The Holy Spirit was undoubtedly leading this poor widow. The Law was not leading her; she could not have been; there was no coin small enough for her to give a tithe of what she had. She gave all that she had and trusted God. Her offering impressed Jesus!

Another (of many) New Testament example is found in 2 Corinthians 8:1-5. In this passage, Paul commends the Macedonians for giving abundantly out of their "deep poverty."

> *"Moreover, brethren, we do you to wit of the grace of God bestowed on the churches of Macedonia; (2) How that in a great trial of affliction the abundance of their joy and their deep poverty abounded unto the riches of their liberality."*
> (2 Corinthians 8:1-2)

The research conducted for this book revealed not a single example of a man or woman of God being led by the Holy Spirit to violate the principle of tithing. Instead, all of God's Word shows that the Holy Spirit **ALWAYS** leads God's people to **go beyond** the minimum requirements of the Law!

The second question - Does the Bible ever speak disparagingly about tithing? **Never!** Our study is unable to find a single negative comment in either Testament about the tithe or tithing. The only negative feedback that can be found is concerning **NOT TITHING** when one should, or by the recipients of the tithes abusing the tithes (see Malachi chapter 3).

Some might quote Matthew 23:23 as an example of the Bible, saying something negative about tithing. However, one should read this passage carefully to understand what it means.

> *"Woe unto you, scribes and Pharisees, hypocrites! for **ye pay tithe** of mint and anise and cummin, and have omitted the weightier matters of the law, judgment, mercy, and faith: **these ought ye to have done**, and not to leave the other undone."*
> (Matthew 23:23, emphasis added)

Before we examine this verse, let's look at Matthew 23:1 and Matthew 23:3, which are critical to understanding the context of verse 23:

> *"Then spake Jesus to the **multitude**, and to **his disciples**,"* (Matthew 23:1)

> *"**All therefore whatsoever they bid you observe, that observe and do**; but do not ye after their works: for they say, and do not."* (Matthew 23:3)

The following are some observations from verses 1 and 3.

* Jesus was speaking to the multitude and His disciples. It is very important to keep this in mind as you read the rest of the chapter. While Jesus is pronouncing "Woes" upon the religious leaders, He is also teaching everyone around Him.

* Verse 3 is rarely taught in God's Kingdom today; Jesus tells His disciples and the multitude that they should obey everything that the teachers of the Law, the scribes and Pharisees taught! Jesus told everyone that they ought to obey the Law. Part of the Law dealt with tithing.

Then in verse 23, Jesus rebukes the religious leaders NOT for tithing, but rather for neglecting **"…the weightier matters of the law, judgment, mercy, and faith…"** Jesus tells them that they should have tithed, but they should not have ignored these more essential things.

"…these ought ye to have done, and not to leave the other undone."

Thus, it is unwise and out of context to say that Jesus spoke disparagingly about tithing. He commended tithing and rebuked the hypocrisy of ignoring the more essential matters of the Law.

(Note: Jesus' comments about obedience to the Law will be clarified in later chapters. In Matthew 5, Jesus said that all had not yet been fulfilled; therefore, our New Covenant obedience is to be based in love and led by the Holy Spirit.)

The third question - Are there examples in the Bible, in either the Old or New Testaments, of the Holy Spirit leading anyone to violate the Law of God, or to do less than the Law required? No, there are not.

> *"Do we then make void the law through faith? **God forbid**: yea, we establish the law."* (Romans 3:31, the Apostle Paul speaking to the Church in New Testament times.)

Most assuredly, there are **no** Bible passages that reveal the Holy Spirit leading anyone to break God's Law! Would the Holy Spirit write the Law and then lead Christians to violate the Law He wrote? **Inconceivable!**

The religious leaders frequently tried to trap Jesus and accuse Him of breaking the Law. These allegations were particularly evident concerning the Sabbath Day. The following passage (and others) show that they were never successful with this accusation since Jesus could further expound God's Word to them, and reveal their hypocrisy.

Read Matthew 12:1-14. Below are excerpts:

> *"...Jesus went on the Sabbath...and his disciples were an hungred, and began to pluck the ears of corn and to eat. (2)...the Pharisees...said...thy disciples do that which is not lawful...(3) But he said unto them, Have ye not read what David did...(4) How he entered into the house of God, and did eat the shewbread, which was not lawful...(5) Or...the priests in the temple profane the sabbath, and are blameless?... (8) For the Son of man is Lord even of the sabbath day. (9)...he went into their synagogue: (10) And, behold, there was a man which had his hand withered. And they asked him, saying, Is it lawful to heal on the sabbath days? that they might accuse him. (11) And he said unto them, What man shall there be among you, that shall have one sheep, and if it fall into a pit on the sabbath day, will he not lay hold on it, and lift it out? (12)...Wherefore it is lawful to do well on the sabbath days. (13) Then saith he to the man, Stretch forth thine hand. And he stretched it forth; and it was restored whole, like as the other..."*
> (Matthew 12:1-14)

Both Matthew 4:1 and Luke 4:1 tell us that Jesus was led by the Holy Spirit.

"And Jesus being full of the Holy Ghost returned from Jordan, and was led by the Spirit into the wilderness," (Luke 4:1)

Since Jesus was led by the Holy Spirit and Himself kept the Law, shouldn't we follow His example in giving, as in all things, being led by the Holy Spirit?

<u>Chapter 3 – Give As You Purpose In Your Heart</u>

> *"Every man according **as he purposeth in his heart, so let him give**; not grudgingly, or of necessity: for God loveth a cheerful giver."*
> (2 Corinthians 9:7, emphasis added)

Give as you **purpose** in your heart in modern Christianity often means giving little or nothing on **purpose!**

The verse above is often cited by those who oppose the teachings on tithing. They surmise that we need only give what we have decided in our hearts to give; therefore, tithing does not pertain to believers (being under the notion that the Law is no longer relevant to Christians.)

While we are no longer under the Law's judgment or condemnation for sin because of grace, Jesus did tell us that not one jot or tittle of the Law would pass away until all has been fulfilled. One key to properly comprehending the Law is in understanding what has already been accomplished, what Jesus is currently achieving in us, and what will yet be fulfilled.

However, taking a single verse out of its context often leads to wrong conclusions, as is the case with the above passage. For example, let's look at the verse right before this one.

> *"But this I say, He which soweth sparingly shall reap also sparingly; and he which soweth bountifully shall reap also bountifully."*
> (2 Corinthians 9:6)

It is fascinating to note that Paul tells us to give as we purpose in our heart **immediately after** teaching that if we offer only a little, we will receive little, and if we give abundantly, we will receive much. Paul was indeed a master of driving home his point. It plays out like this:

* If you give a little, you get a little,
* If you give much, you get much,
* Decide in your heart whether you want to receive little or much and give that cheerfully!

Is Paul telling his audience to give whatever they want? Or is Paul instructing them regarding God's faithfulness and encouraging them to give **bountifully**? Think back to the widow's mite again: that little lady not only gave bountifully (all she had), she exercised great faith, understanding that God had given generously to her and would continue to take care of her. That is what faithful giving is all about.

As one reads this entire chapter in 2 Corinthians, it becomes even more evident that verse 7 is **not** permission to give less than a tithe. Throughout this chapter, Paul makes it clear that God's people should give generously back to God, with the biblical expectation that God's unfailing generosity will continue to be bestowed upon them. Paul is not an advocate of giving little!

> *"For it is superfluous for me to write to you about this ministry to the saints; (2) for I know your readiness, of which I boast about you to the Macedonians, namely, that Achaia has been prepared* [with a gift] *since last year, and your zeal has stirred up most of them."*
> (2 Corinthians 9:1-2 NASB)

Vs. 1-2: In these verses, Paul boasts to the Macedonians about the Corinthians' eagerness to give. Paul also notes that the Corinthians' enthusiasm for giving had resulted in stirring the Macedonians to similar action!

> *"And let us consider one another to provoke unto love and to good works:"* (Hebrews 10:24)

> *"But I have sent the brethren, in order that our boasting about you may not be made empty in this case, so that, as I was saying, you may be prepared; (4) otherwise if any Macedonians come with me and find you unprepared, we—not to speak of you—will be put to shame by this confidence. (5) So I thought it necessary to urge the brethren that they would go on ahead to you and arrange beforehand your previously promised bountiful gift, so that the same would be ready as a bountiful gift and not affected by covetousness."* (2 Corinthians 9:3-5)

Vs. 3-5: Paul sends brothers to Corinth in advance to make sure that they are ready to give as they had promised, and to finalize the details of their generous gift. The Corinthian church had given generously in the past, and Paul is attempting to ensure that their next generous donation will be ready. Paul wanted to be sure that his boasting to the Macedonians was not unfounded, nor his confidence in the Corinthians to be misplaced. These verses certainly don't lend themselves to modern concepts of *give whatever you want*.

> *"And God is able to make all grace abound toward you; that ye, always having all sufficiency in all things, may abound to every good work: (9) (As it is written, He hath dispersed abroad; he hath given to the poor: his righteousness remaineth for ever."*
> (2 Corinthians 9:8-9)

Vs. 8-9: We have discussed verses 6 and 7 previously; therefore, we will now consider verses 8 and 9. In verse 8, Paul instructs us that God can bless us abundantly so that in all things, we have what we need. These blessings are to provide for us that we may also abound in every good work. Verse 8 must be taken in context with verse 6: that if we give little, we will be blessed little. The expectation is "all sufficiency in all things" and that they may "abound," the context is that which arises from abundant giving.

> *"He hath dispersed, he hath given to the poor; his righteousness endureth for ever; his horn shall be exalted with honour."* (Psalm 112:9)

In 2 Corinthians 9:9, Paul quotes Psalm 112:9. From this quotation, Paul emphasizes **freely** scattering their gifts to the poor. In 2 Corinthians 9:9, Paul uses the Greek word (skorpizō) translated as "He hath dispersed abroad," which is defined as "to dissipate...be liberal" (Strong's Concordance G4650). Paul is stressing generosity.

Their gifting seems to be repeatedly above and beyond mere tithes. And Paul reminds us that God will bless us abundantly and meet all our needs. We are told to scatter our gifts to the poor freely. As one reads the context of 2 Corinthians chapter 9, it becomes more and more difficult to defend a position of giving less than a tithe.

> *"Now he that ministereth seed to the sower both minister bread for your food, and multiply your seed sown, and increase the fruits of your righteousness; (11) Being enriched in every thing to all bountifulness, which causeth through us thanksgiving to God."* (2 Corinthians 9:10-11)

Vs. 10-11: In these verses, Paul continues the thought of God's abundant provision. Paul teaches the various and wonderful ways in which God will enrich us, enabling us to be generous all the time, and His generosity will lead to thanksgiving unto God.

This big-heartedness is exemplified by the story of the widow's mites in Mark 12:41-44. Jesus was not impressed with the rich people giving their tithes and offerings; He was impressed with the poor widow giving 100% of the money she possessed. Jesus was so impressed that He called His disciples over and showed them what was happening. Undoubtedly this generosity (which impressed Jesus) led to thanksgiving towards God!

> *"For the administration of this service not only supplieth the want of the saints, but is abundant also by many thanksgivings unto God; (13) Whiles by the experiment of this ministration they glorify God for your professed subjection unto the gospel of Christ, and for your liberal distribution unto them, and unto all men; (14) And by their prayer for you, which long after you for the exceeding grace of God in you. (15) Thanks be unto God for his unspeakable gift."* (2 Corinthians 9:12-15)

2 Corinthians 9:12-15: These verses represent Paul's summary regarding the results of the Corinthians' generosity. Here is an overview of this summary:

* Verse 12 – supplies the needs of the Lord's people,
* Verse 12 – overflows in expressions of thankfulness,
* Verse 13 – proves their obedience and their faith in Jesus,
* Verse 13 – others will praise God,
* Verse 14 – those who are blessed will pray for you,

* Verse 14 – recognition of God's exceeding grace, and desiring for themselves more of the great grace of God they see in you,
* Verse 15 – thanks to God for His unspeakable gift.

Can we honestly believe that these abundant and liberally distributed blessings could result from God's people giving less than a tithe? Can we honestly consider giving as one *purposes in their heart* means giving just a little bit or nothing?

We must always consider the context of the entire passage. When reviewing 2 Corinthians chapter 9, it is impossible to imagine that Paul was encouraging Christians to give what they want, if that idea meant giving less than tithes.

Chapter 4 - Grace Always Exceeds The Law!

> *"For I say unto you, That except **your righteousness shall exceed** the righteousness of the scribes and Pharisees, ye shall in no case enter into the kingdom of heaven."* (Matthew 5:20)

The notion of grace allowing us to do less than the Law requires is foreign to the Bible. God's grace includes His Holy Spirit living within us. God's grace far exceeds the Law!

Righteousness is a great place to start. In Matthew 5:20, quoted above, we see that our righteousness must exceed that which comes via the Law. This statement alone demonstrates that the requirements of grace are far superior to those of the Law!

How is this evidenced in the Bible?

* Paul said that regarding the righteousness of the Law, he was "blameless" (see Philippians 3:6),

* This righteousness is "filthy rags" and "dung" (see Isaiah 64:6 and Philippians 3:8),

* The righteousness of grace is the righteousness of Jesus Christ Himself imputed to us! Of course, this righteousness **FAR** exceeds that which comes from the Law!

> *"Simon Peter, a servant and an apostle of Jesus Christ, to them that have obtained like precious faith with us through the **righteousness of God** and our Saviour Jesus Christ:"* (2 Peter 1:1)

*"Even the **righteousness of God** which is by faith of Jesus Christ unto all and upon all them that believe: for there is no difference:"* (Romans 3:22)

At this point, some might say, "See, this is why the Law was done away with, it could not save us!" But this is to miss the point, which is simply this: **Grace SURPASSES the Law!**

Aside from our righteousness, how does this apply to everyday life?

The Matthew 5 verses that follow verse 20 provide further clarification and demonstrations of how the righteousness of grace exceeds the Law. Here are a few examples:

The Law: Thou shalt not kill.
Grace: Thou shalt not be unjustly angry with a brother.

> *"Ye have heard that it was said of them of old time, **Thou shalt not kill**; and whosoever shall kill shall be in danger of the judgment: (22) But I say unto you, That **whosoever is angry with his brother without a cause** shall be in danger of the judgment: and whosoever shall say to his brother, Raca, shall be in danger of the council: but whosoever shall say, Thou fool, shall be in danger of hell fire."* (Matthew 5:21-22)

This passage clearly shows that the necessities of grace go beyond the mandates of the Law. In the Law, murder places one in danger of the judgment. Grace sets one who is angry with a brother without cause in danger of the judgment.

The Law: Thou shalt not commit adultery.

Grace: Thou shalt not lust.

> *"Ye have heard that it was said by them of old time,* ***Thou shalt not commit adultery****: (28) But I say unto you,* ***That whosoever looketh on a woman to lust*** *after her hath committed adultery with her already in his heart."* (Matthew 5:27-28)

Again, these Scriptures make it clear that grace surpasses the Law. The Law defines and forbids the physical actions, whereas grace, exposes, and condemns the heart of the person.

The Law: Thou shalt love thy neighbor and hate your enemy.

Grace: Thou shalt love your enemies, bless those that curse you, do good to them that hate you, and pray for those who persecute you.

> *"Ye have heard that it hath been said,* ***Thou shalt love thy neighbour, and hate thine enemy****. (44) But I say unto you,* ***Love your enemies****, bless them that curse you, do good to them that hate you, and pray for them which despitefully use you, and persecute you;"* (Matthew 5:43-44)

Jesus Christ makes it very clear that the requirements of His righteousness are far above those of the Law! The good news is this, Jesus has given us the Holy Spirit to help us live out these requirements of grace. And the Blood of Jesus has been shed to provide reconciliation every time that we fail to be led by God's Spirit, every time we sin.

God's expectations with regards to the moral Laws is that we OBEY THEM!

How does this apply to giving tithes?

The Law: Thou shalt give tithes for the purposes of God.
Grace: 100% belongs to God! Therefore, we need to be faithful in the little things (tithing), and God will give us additional stewardship.

> *"But this I say, He which **soweth sparingly shall reap also sparingly**; and he which **soweth bountifully shall reap also bountifully**. (7) Every man according as he purposeth in his heart, so let him give; not grudgingly, or of necessity: for God loveth a cheerful giver. (8) And God is able to make all grace abound toward you; that ye, always having all sufficiency in all things, may abound to every good work:"* (2 Corinthians 9:6-8)

> *"As a result of your ministry, they will give glory to God. **For your generosity** to them and to all believers **will prove that you are obedient to the Good News of Christ**."* (2 Corinthians 9:13 NLT)

Paul associates **abundant and generous giving** with **obedience to the Gospel of Christ**. If we are in bondage and unable to tithe, how can we be free to abundantly and generously give?

Chapter 5 - Jesus Teaches Tithing – Part 1

*"Then spake Jesus to the multitude, and to his disciples, (2) Saying The scribes and the Pharisees sit in Moses' seat: (3) **All therefore whatsoever they bid you observe**, that observe and do; but do not ye after their works: for they say, and do not."* (Matthew 23:1-3)

*"Woe unto you, scribes and Pharisees, hypocrites! for ye **pay tithe** of mint and anise and cummin, and have omitted the weightier matters of the law, judgment, mercy, and faith: **these ought ye to have done**, and not to leave the other undone."* (Matthew 23:23)

While it is commonly thought that Jesus did not teach tithing, this chapter (and others in this book) will demonstrate that Jesus did indeed speak of tithing, both directly and indirectly.

In this chapter, we will be revisiting a few verses in Matthew 23.

Important Observations (from the verses quoted above):

* Verse 1 tells us who Jesus was addressing. It is crucial to note that He was teaching the **multitudes** AND His **disciples**. Some people will try to dismiss this discourse of Jesus with the idea that this chapter is merely a criticism of the religious leaders, but this Scripture makes it clear as to whom Jesus was speaking.

* In verse 3, Jesus tells His disciples and the multitude to observe and obey ALL that the scribes and Pharisees teach that they should do, which included tithing.

* In verse 3, Jesus also tells the multitude and His disciples to avoid the hypocrisy of the scribes and Pharisees.

* In verse 23, Jesus says that the scribes and Pharisees pay tithes but ignore the more important things. He emphasizes that they **SHOULD** pay their tithes, but they should **NOT** neglect the "weightier matters of the law."

Since Matthew 23 is replete with condemnation of the religious leaders' double standards, it is very easy to miss the few positive things that are said. The scribes and Pharisees are very clearly hypocrites, and Jesus does not make any attempt to "sugar coat" this fact.

However, there are a few often-overlooked teachings of Jesus in this chapter. We will examine a couple of these as they pertain to tithing.

The first is surprising. Jesus tells His disciples and the multitude that they should **OBEY ALL** that the scribes and Pharisees teach! Wow!

Why would Jesus say such a thing? Simply, these religious leaders were teaching the TRUTH of God's Word. Therefore, we should obey it!

The scribes and Pharisees taught the Law; therefore, they certainly instructed with regards to tithing. So below is the scenario:

* Jesus told the people to obey the teachings of the scribes and Pharisees.

* They taught tithing (as well as the rest of the Law).

* Therefore, Jesus taught obedience to the Law regarding tithing.

In Matthew 23:23, Jesus makes this even more clear. Read this verse carefully.

Jesus does NOT rebuke the scribes and Pharisees for paying tithes. He DOES rebuke them for ignoring the more critical aspects of the Law (judgment, mercy, and faith).

Jesus tells the religious leaders that they **SHOULD pay their tithes**, but that they SHOULD NOT neglect these more essential matters.

In summary, we see Jesus instructing His disciples and the multitude to obey the teachings of the scribes and Pharisees. We see Him telling the scribes and Pharisees that they should tithe. We see Him telling everyone not to be hypocritical and to pay closer attention to the "weightier matters of the law."

Viewing this passage as a condemnation of tithing by Jesus is to ignore the context and His very words. While, as is the case with this passage, there are negative references in the Bible to scribes and Pharisees, there are no passages that speak disparagingly about tithing.

Chapter 6 - Jesus Teaches Tithing – Part 2

*"And seeing the **multitudes**, he went up into a mountain: and when he was set, **his disciples** came unto him:"* (Matthew 5:1)

*"Think **not** that I am come to **destroy the law**, or the prophets: I am not come to destroy, but to fulfil. (18) For verily I say unto you, **Till heaven and earth pass, one jot or one tittle shall in no wise pass from the law, till all be fulfilled.** (19) Whosoever therefore shall break one of these least commandments, and shall teach men so, he shall be called the least in the kingdom of heaven: but whosoever shall do and teach them, the same shall be called great in the kingdom of heaven."*
(Matthew 5:17-19)

This chapter continues the examination of Jesus' teaching regarding tithing, in the context of the Law. We will look at what Jesus says regarding the Law.

Again, it is essential to take note of whom Jesus is addressing. Verse 1 tells us that He was once again teaching the multitudes and His disciples.

Important Observations:

* Jesus clearly states that He has **NOT** come to destroy the Law and the Prophets (verse 17).

* Verse 17 also tells us that Jesus came to fulfill the Law and the Prophets.

* In verse 18, Jesus says that **NOT ONE** jot or tittle of the Law will be done away with **until heaven and earth pass away**, and all be fulfilled.

* Jesus tells us in verse 19 that anyone who breaks one of the least of these commandments and teaches others also to violate the Law, they will be the least in the kingdom of heaven. Those who obey and teach the Law will be great in the kingdom of heaven.

We will look at these Bible verses about the Law in the light of giving tithes. Tithing is a part of the Law; therefore, statements of Jesus about the Law apply to the commands about tithing.

Jesus definitively states (verse 17) that His purpose did not include the destruction of the Law and Prophets, but it was to fulfill them. Jesus fulfilling the Law is very interesting since verse 18 says that no aspect of the Law will be done away with until "all be fulfilled."

The common argument is that Jesus has already fulfilled all things; therefore, the Law is passed away. This thinking sounds good, but is it accurate? Verse 18 also says that no part of the Law will be done away with **until heaven and earth pass away**. Since heaven and earth have not passed away yet, the Law is still in place (every jot and tittle).

Jesus was speaking to both His disciples and to the multitudes as to what they should be doing. If He'd intended for them only to be doing so until His resurrection, wouldn't He have said so?

So, we must ask the following, "Has **all** been fulfilled already?" The obvious answer is **<u>NO</u>!**

Jesus has not yet returned in the second coming. We do not yet have glorified spiritual bodies, nor are we yet living eternally in the Presence of God. Heaven and earth have not yet passed away. As is abundantly evident from these few examples promised in the Scripture, there is **still MUCH** that needs to be fulfilled.

So what about Jesus fulfilling all the Law and the Prophets? Absolutely, in Jesus Christ all things will be satisfied!

Some things have already been fulfilled. ALL of the Law that pertains to sacrifices for sin has ALREADY been wholly fulfilled in Jesus Christ! ALL of the Law that relates to the penalties for sin has ALREADY been completely fulfilled in Jesus Christ!

We will look at some aspects of the Law in the next chapter. It is critical to understand that everything from the Law and the Prophets has not yet been fulfilled.

For example, "Thou shalt not kill." Has this aspect of the Law been completely satisfied? Does God still expect His people to OBEY this Law? Of course! What about lying? Does God still expect us to tell the truth? Of course! How about coveting? Does God expect us not to covet our neighbor's spouse or possessions? Of course!

Jesus Himself personally fulfilled all aspects of the Law. He was completely obedient.

So then, does God still expect us to obey the unfulfilled aspects of the Law? Of course!

Is tithing part of the Law? Yes. Does God expect us to tithe? God expects us to be led by the Holy Spirit, Who will never lcad us to disobey God's Word.

Here's the thing: the only way that God would no longer expect us to exercise the principles of giving in the tithe would be if that aspect of the Law were already fulfilled. Tithing laws were primarily set up to make provision for those who ministered in God's work. Since we still have people who minister in the work of the Lord, is it possible that this part of the Law has been completely fulfilled?

The next chapter will review some of the various aspects of the Law. We will see where tithing fits into these aspects, and understand why this principle of giving is still in place. The Holy Spirit will lead and empower us to give abundantly and generously!

Chapter 7 – Understanding The Law

*"For verily I say unto you, **Till heaven and earth pass**, one jot or one tittle shall in no wise pass from the law, till all be fulfilled."* (Matthew 5:18)

In the previous chapter, we began to review the different aspects of the Law God gave to Moses. It is very important to have some understanding of these aspects to understand why God still holds us accountable for lying, for example, but does not hold us responsible for sacrificing sheep. Therefore, in this chapter, we will look at a brief overview of these aspects of the Law.

At this point, we should make it clear that the Bible does not specifically breakdown the Law of Moses into the following various aspects. However, to assist in understanding what parts of the Law have not yet been fully completed (since Heaven and earth have not yet passed away), the following categories will be helpful.

The Law of Moses has been categorized in many different ways, so researching this subject may lead one to different designations. However, the list below will serve the purpose of this book.

* Sacrificial Laws – These laws pertain to the various sacrifices for sin,

* Penal Laws – These laws pertain to the various penalties for sin,

* Temple / Ceremonial Laws – These laws pertain to the ceremonies surrounding the Temple,

* Moral Laws – These laws pertain to <u>interactions between people</u>.

When reading the above, it should be immediately apparent to Christians why some aspects of the Law have already been completely fulfilled. Below we will briefly discuss these categories.

Sacrificial Laws

> *"By the which will we are sanctified through the* ***offering of the body of Jesus Christ once for all****."* (Hebrews 10:10)

The Bible tells us that Jesus is the final and only valid sacrifice for sin. The death, burial, and resurrection of Jesus, the Messiah, is the COMPLETE FULFILLMENT of all sacrificial laws. No more sacrifice for sin is ever needed. Therefore, the Sacrificial Laws have been completely fulfilled in Jesus, the Messiah!

Penal Laws

> *"Ye are* ***bought with a price****; be not ye the servants of men."* (1 Corinthians 7:23)

The penalties for sin have been likewise wholly fulfilled in Jesus' death, burial, and resurrection. If we look at Hebrews 10:10 and First Corinthians 7:23 (both referenced above), we can see that the penalty for our sin has been paid. **Jesus paid it all!** Therefore, the Penal Laws have been completely fulfilled in Jesus, the Messiah!

Temple / Ceremonial Laws

> *"But he spake of the* ***temple of his body****."*

(John 2:21)

*"What? know ye not that **your body is the temple of the Holy Ghost** which is in you, which ye have of God, and ye are not your own?"* (Corinthians 6:19)

From the above Scripture passages, we can understand that the Temple or Ceremonial Laws no longer have an application to the physical Temple building, because upon Jesus' resurrection, He was the rebuilt Temple, and His body is that of which He spoke. We are also instructed that Christians are now the Temple of the Holy Spirit, Who lives in us.

The Laws of Moses that applied to the Temple and the actions therein are not directly applicable to believers in Jesus Christ. There may be spiritual correlations between the physical Temple and the New Covenant Temple. Still, direct applications have been completely fulfilled in the resurrection of Jesus and the indwelling of the Holy Spirit.

Moral Laws

Finally, we have come to the parts of the Law of Moses that are still yet to be fulfilled entirely. Because of the Holy Spirit dwelling in us, God expects and empowers us to fulfill these laws daily. What are some examples of these moral laws?

* We should love the Lord our God with all our heart, soul, strength and mind, and our neighbor as ourselves,
* We should not murder,
* We should not covet,
* We should not lie,
* We should not steal,
* We should not rob from God (Tithing principle).

Most Christians who oppose the principle of tithing would agree with all of these moral laws until you get to the last one. They would likely try to classify robbing from God as a ceremonial law.

It seems strange that some Christians would condemn robbing from others, yet dismiss robbing from God as no longer being valid.

Would the tithing principle qualify as a ceremonial or moral law? Once we look at God's intended purpose for the tithe, we see that it serves a moral purpose. That purpose is to provide for the Old Testament priests as payment for their ministry work. Here is what God says is His purpose for the tithes:

> *"And, behold, I have given the children of Levi all the tenth in Israel for an inheritance, **for their service which they serve, even the service of the tabernacle of the congregation.**"* (Numbers 18:21)

God makes it clear that the tithe was intended for the provision of those He called into His ministry. God's stated purpose is to pay His servants for their ministry service.

Tithing is a moral law. **If you were not paid for your work, you would consider that to be immoral!** It is the same for God's called ministers. The Apostle Paul understood this concept when he compared the Temple priests with Gospel preachers.

> *"Do ye not know that they which minister about holy things live of the things of the temple? and they which wait at the altar are partakers with the altar?*

*(14) Even so **hath the Lord ordained that they which preach the gospel should live of the gospel**.*"
(1 Corinthians 9:13-14)

Did Jesus die on the Cross to allow us to violate God's Law? We will let the Apostle Paul answer this question:

> *"What then? **shall we sin**, because we are not under the law, but under grace? **God forbid**."*
> (Romans 6:15)

The above verse may appear evident to Christians. Few would make allowances for sin, but what is God's definition of sin in the New Testament?

> *"... for sin is the transgression of the law."*
> (1 John 3:4)

Lastly, when Paul made his defense before the governor in Acts chapter 24, we see further that Paul understood Jesus' words regarding the jots and tittles of the Law. Paul said:

> *"But this I confess unto thee, that after the way which they call heresy, so worship I the God of my fathers, **believing all things which are written in the law and in the prophets:**"* (Acts 24:14)

Chapter 8 – NT Giving: The Poor Widow

*"And Jesus sat over against the treasury, and **beheld** how the people **cast money into the treasury**: and many that were **rich cast in much**. (42) And there came a certain **poor widow**, and she threw in two mites, which make a farthing. (43) And **he called unto him his disciples**, and saith unto them, Verily I say unto you, That this **poor widow hath cast more in, than all they** which have cast into the treasury: (44) For all they did cast in of their abundance; but **she of her want did cast in all that she had, even all her living**."* (Mark 12:41-44)

Remember, God's ways are **not** our ways!

When discussing tithing, many Christians embrace a notion that goes something like the following.

Poor people who can barely pay their rent or put food on the table should give little or nothing, and wealthy people should give more. While this sounds loving and kind, it does not reflect the way that Jesus views things. This concept more closely follows specific political thought patterns than that of the Bible. This thinking robs God, the church, and the giver of His blessings that derive from giving.

Here is what the Bible says about the rich giving more and the poor less:

*"The **rich shall not give more**, and the **poor shall not give less** than half a shekel, **when they give an offering unto the LORD**, to make an atonement for your souls."* (Exodus 30:15)

32

Let's look at what Jesus says about the poor widow's giving.

Re-read the passage from Mark cited at the top of this chapter and note the details. We see that Jesus "beheld" how people cast their money into the treasury. The word "beheld" is even more interesting when we look at the definition of the Greek word that is used. The following is from the Strong's Concordance.

beheld = Strong's G2334 – "theōreō - to be a spectator, look at, behold - to view attentively, take a view of, survey - to view mentally, consider"

Jesus was not merely looking at what was going on. He was carefully surveying the monetary activity at the treasury. Jesus knew what was about to happen, and He was awaiting this opportunity to teach regarding faith and faithfulness. **It was a chance to let His disciples see the way that He saw things.**

Jesus watched the wealthy throw in large sums of money, and then He saw this poor widow come. She threw in two mites, almost nothing, which seems to be right in line with modern thought that the rich should give more, and the poor should give less.

However, Jesus is not in sync with this philosophy! Jesus is so impressed with this poor woman's contribution that He calls His disciples over to show them. **Jesus brags to His disciples about this woman's faithful generosity.** He says that she gave more than all the rest.

This woman was so in love with God that she gave 100% of the money she had to Him. Her faithfulness and trust impressed Jesus so much that He had to show it to His disciples.

If this woman had not been faithful in her giving (100% of what she had), we would not have this incredible story that demonstrates one way that we can impress Jesus. Praise the Lord; this woman did not listen to those who may have told her to stay home and not give anything (as many would teach her in modern Christianity).

So the question is, "Will you be the one to tell the poor not to give? Not to support the work of the Lord?" Or will you teach them to give faithfully and see God's excellent provision in their own lives? The poor widow gave **far beyond** the minimum requirements of the Law!

> *"Whosoever therefore shall break one of these least commandments, and shall teach men so, he shall be called the least in the kingdom of heaven: but whosoever shall do and teach them, the same shall be called great in the kingdom of heaven."* (Matthew 5:19)

Chapter 9 - NT Giving: The Macedonians

"Now, brethren, we wish to make known to you the **grace of God** *which has been given in the* **churches of Macedonia**, *(2) that in a* **great ordeal of affliction** *their* **abundance of joy** *and their* **deep poverty** *overflowed in the* **wealth of their liberality**. *(3) For I testify that according to their ability, and* **beyond their ability**, *they gave of their own accord, (4)* **begging us** *with* **much urging** *for the favor of participation in the support of the saints, (5) and this, not as we had expected, but they first* **gave themselves to the Lord** *and* **to us** *by the* **will of God**." (2 Corinthians 8:1-5 - NASB)

The above is a fantastic example of New Testament giving. After reading accounts such as this, the widow and her two mites, the generosity of the first church, and others, it is difficult to believe that there are still those who teach that the Holy Spirit will lead people to do less than the minimums of the Law. There are NO Bible examples of Holy Spirit-led people breaking the Law. The Holy Spirit empowers us to exceed the minimums of the Law by far.

As we review this passage, ponder the notion of giving less than a tithe. Look at this example and other New Testament examples, then try to find room for being led by the Holy Spirit and giving little or nothing. It seems unfathomable that God would lead people to violate the Law He gave to Moses. If you looked into the New Testament for such examples, you'd find that no such precedent exists in the Bible.

The Apostle Paul is relating the generosity of the Macedonians as a testimonial to the Corinthians. We will see in the next chapter (2 Corinthians 9), Paul spoke to the

Macedonians of the generosity of the Corinthians. **Paul desires generous giving from both**, and uses the witness of each to spur the other group on to love and good works.

Observations from the Macedonians:
* Paul emphasizes the "grace of God,"
* The Macedonians were in a "great ordeal of affliction,"
* The Macedonians experienced an "abundance of joy,"
* The Macedonians were in "deep poverty,"
* The Macedonians expressed "wealth of their liberality,"
* The Macedonians gave willingly, "beyond their ability,"
* The Macedonians BEGGED to give in "support of the saints,"
* The Macedonians gave themselves first "to the Lord,"
* The Macedonians then gave themselves to Paul by the "will of God."

These descriptions are an incredible testament to the Macedonians. They REALLY loved Jesus, and Paul says that it showed! Below, we will look briefly at each of these bullet points.

Paul emphasizes the "grace of God"

Paul was fully aware that the only way the Macedonians could respond in this manner is by Christ living in and through them. The grace of God motivated and enabled them to trust Him. Having said this, Paul was also aware that God is no respecter of persons and makes His grace available to all.

Therefore, the Macedonians acted upon the grace of God. Most Christians today do not trust God like this. Seriously, how many people do you know who BEG to give to the ministries God has ordained? Paul's appeal to the "grace of God" in this case reminds one of this saying:

Without God… we CAN'T! Without us… He WON'T!

The Macedonians were in a "great ordeal of affliction"

By definition, a "great ordeal of affliction" can be understood as a large testing of one's character and faith under intense pressure. In this case, the Macedonian's abounding generosity is evidence that they passed the test! Here are the Greek words God chose to use, and their definitions:

a great - Strong's G4183 - "polys - many, much, large"

ordeal - Strong's G1382 - "dokimē - proving, trial – approved, tried character - a proof, a specimen of tried worth"

of affliction - Strong's G2347 – "thlipsis - a pressing, pressing together, pressure - metaph. oppression, affliction, tribulation, distress, straits"

Since the Bible tells us that the love of money is the root of all sorts of evil, it is not surprising that many tests of the Christian faith come in the form of finances. The very first problem in the early church was over money (we will look at this in a later chapter.)

The Macedonians faith was being tried, and they were powerfully passing the test! Can anyone imagine a similar testimony from a group of people who were not generous? No such examples are to be found in the pages of the Bible.

The Macedonians experienced an "abundance of joy"

God's ways indeed are not our ways! When we are in severe afflictions and deep poverty, an abundance of joy is not what we expect our expression to be. So, where did the Macedonians obtain such overwhelming joy? The same place that is available to us, trusting in God! Really trusting in God!

> *"Thou wilt keep him in **perfect peace**, whose mind is stayed on thee: because **he trusteth in thee**."* (Isaiah 26:3)

> *"Whom having not seen, ye love; in whom, though now ye see him not, **yet believing, ye rejoice with joy unspeakable and full of glory**:"* (1 Peter 1:8)

The unimaginable generosity of the Macedonians is an exemplary result of truly trusting in Jesus. They were experiencing the joy of the Lord as they trusted Him and saw His great faithfulness. One must wonder if this group would have been mentioned in the Bible if they gave LESS than the minimum requirements of the Law or nothing at all.

The Macedonians were in "deep poverty"

Similar to the poor widow who gave 100% of what she had, all her living, these Macedonians defy human logic and again prove that God's ways are not ours. Like the widow, people would have told them to use their money to take care of their families. This thinking is the wisdom of humanity that the rich should give more, and the poor should give less.

Is it possible to conceive that these Macedonians or the poor widow would have been better off following the worldly concept of letting the rich give, and use the little you have for yourself? Spirit-led giving is abundantly beyond the requirements of the Law.

The Macedonians expressed "wealth of their liberality"

The "wealth of their liberality" means that the Macedonians were not selfish, nor were they giving with any pretense. They did not give to gain anything, no name, no fame, nothing. They gave out of an open heart of love, which flowed out in generosity! Here are definitions of two of these Greek words:

the wealth - Strong's G4149 – "ploutos - riches, wealth - abundance of external possessions - fulness, abundance, plenitude"

liberality - Strong's G572 – "haplotēs - singleness, simplicity, sincerity, mental honesty - the virtue of one who is free from pretense and hypocrisy - not self-seeking, openness of heart manifesting itself by generosity"

These people possessed an abundant wealth of generosity, which is the earmark of New Testament giving in each and every Bible example wherein God was pleased.

The Macedonians gave willingly, "beyond their ability"

Extravagant generosity is exactly what Holy Spirit-led giving is like, beyond our ability!

Anyone can give a tithe within the power of their ability. Only the Holy Spirit can empower someone to give 100% of their living (the widow) or out of their deep poverty and severe afflictions (the Macedonians).

Is it even plausible to think that a Christian who is led by the Holy Spirit would be too weak to meet the minimums of the Law?

The Macedonians BEGGED to give in "support of the saints"

Has any reader ever heard anyone BEG to donate? We are all too familiar with "ministries" that beg for donations, but to beg to give!

This intense desire to support ministry is an utterly fantastic commentary on what the love of Jesus can do in the hearts of people. It is astounding to see what lives surrendered to Jesus Christ can and will do!

For people in love with Jesus, tithing should not even be a question. Look at the Bible examples of how a real relationship with Jesus impacts people.

The Macedonians gave themselves first "to the Lord"

The utmost importance of giving yourself to the Lord above all is CRITICAL to understand. They first gave themselves to the Lord. People should be encouraged by accounts like this in the Bible. However, we should not attempt to duplicate this unbelievable generosity if we have not truly given ourselves to Jesus. This type of giving must come out of a life that is walking in the Holy Ghost.

The Macedonians then gave themselves to Paul by the "will of God"

Once these people had given themselves to the Lord, they learned the "will of God." God wanted them to give themselves to Paul.

God has not changed; He still calls His people to **generous giving** to His **legitimate** ministers.

Most assuredly, con-men and charlatans are seeking to fleece the flock of God and devour widows' houses. These imposters are a very genuine concern in the world today. However, the existence of such thieves does not change the facts of the Bible.

The power of the Macedonian testimony should surely spur us on to love and good works, which flows out of love for Jesus and the leading of the Holy Spirit.

Chapter 10 - NT Giving: The Corinthians

*"for I know **your readiness, of which I boast** about you to the Macedonians, namely, that Achaia has been prepared since last year, and **your zeal has stirred up most of them.**"*
(2 Corinthians 9:2 NASB)

In the previous chapter of this book, we learned that Paul wrote to the Corinthians about the unimaginable generosity of the Macedonians (see 2 Corinthians chapter 8). In this chapter, we see that Paul told the Macedonians of the generosity of the Corinthians.

It certainly seems clear that Paul encouraged generous giving, that is, giving substantially beyond the minimum requirements of the Law.

In 2 Corinthians 9, Paul very clearly demonstrates an expectation of generous giving. The content of this chapter is quite amazing if read in full. The lone verse in this chapter (verse 6), when taken in context, can in no way be used to justify giving little or nothing. Here is an overview of the entire chapter:

* Verse 1 - Paul says it is not necessary to write to the Corinthians about giving to the ministry.
* Verse 2 - The Corinthians were very ready to offer, and Paul bragged about their generosity.
* Verse 3 - Paul secures his boasting about the Corinthians' giving by sending brothers in advance to make sure their generous gift was ready upon his arrival.
* Verse 4 - Paul sent the brothers to assure their preparedness to give so that neither he nor the Corinthians would be ashamed, in case anyone from Macedonia came to Corinth with Paul.

* Verse 5 - For the reason stated in verse 4, Paul felt it necessary to have the brothers go on ahead to prepare the Corinthians bountiful gift for his arrival. He stresses that this preparation is not out of covetousness.

* Verse 6 - This verse is critical to understanding the context of verse 7. Paul says if you give a little, you will reap a little, and if you give abundantly, you will reap abundantly.

* Verse 7 - In the light of verse 6, Paul says that every man should give as he purposes in his heart. There is nothing in the context of this chapter (or the Bible) that allows for Spirit-led minimal or no giving.

* Verse 8 - In the context of generosity, Paul says that God will provide your needs and beyond so that you will have an abundance to be able to minister to every good work.

* Verses 9-10 - Paul quotes the Old Testament in regards to God's faithfulness to those who are generous.

* Verse 11 - Paul says that, in light of their generosity, they will be enriched in everything so that they can continue giving abundantly. Their liberal giving is producing thanksgiving unto God!

* Verse 12 - The giving ministry of the Corinthians is not only supplying for the needs of the saints but is overflowing in many thanksgivings unto God!

* Verse 13 - Paul equates their giving to PROOF of their OBEDIENCE to the Gospel of Jesus Christ.

* Verse 14 - Paul says that the Corinthians' proof of obedience to the Gospel has caused others to pray for them, and recognize the surpassing grace of God in them.

* Verse 15 - Paul closes this chapter thanking God for His unspeakable gift!

In summary: Paul bragged to the Macedonians about how generous the Corinthians were. The Macedonians are spurred on to love and good works and become generous as well. The Corinthians had promised another donation, and just to be sure that Paul's boasting of them was not in vain, he sent brothers ahead to make sure their generous gift was ready upon Paul's arrival.

Let's look at this in modern terms.

Suppose your church supports a missionary. This person boasts of your generosity to other churches. These other churches are encouraged, and likewise, become very generous. Your missionary is scheduled to come to your church. Some members from the other church express a desire to visit with him. Then, to keep himself and your church from being ashamed, the missionary sends others ahead of him to make sure your generous donation is ready when he arrives.

God's ways are not our ways!

With the content and context of this chapter, there is no valid justification for Holy Spirit-led giving to fall below the minimums of the Law, that is, the tithe.

Chapter 11 – NT Giving: The Early Church

> *"**Neither was there any among them that lacked**: for as many as were **possessors of lands or houses sold them, and brought the prices of the things that were sold**, (35) And laid them down at the apostles' feet: and distribution was made unto every man according as he had need."* (Acts 4:34-35)

In the previous chapters, we have seen how a relationship with Jesus made a powerful impact on the poor concerning generous giving. In this chapter, we will examine the Holy Spirit-led giving of the wealthy.

Observations from the passage above:

* No Christian suffered lack,
* All who owned lands or houses sold them,
* The purchase prices were given to the Apostles,
* The donations were distributed as needed.

We will look briefly at each of these observations below to see the application today.

No Christian suffered lack

Wow! There are likely very few fellowships of believers who can claim this statement. Probably every church body has members who are suffering some type of lack. Of course, this is not to say that every Christian should be abounding in wealth, but it is saying that God supplies for the needs of His people, usually through His people.

> *"But **my God shall supply all your need** according to his riches in glory by Christ Jesus."*
> (Philippians 4:19)

God has not changed, and He does not change. We see the Old Testament example of God providing **for** His people **through** His people in the Genesis story of Joseph. A famine covered the land, and Joseph was used by God to provide for His people, Jacob, and his family.

We see the same pattern here in the early church. God provided for those in His Kingdom through others in His Kingdom. In this case, people who had wealth were so moved by the love God showered upon them, that they sold property and gave it to the church leaders, the Apostles. At this point, the Apostles oversaw the distribution of this wealth of donations, and all needs were met!

All who owned lands or houses sold them

As noted above, previous chapters dealt with how God moved the poor to give, in this case, we are seeing the impact of the Holy Spirit's leading on the more well-to-do. In either case, the **Holy Spirit leads to giving in excess!** We find nowhere in the Bible, where the Holy Ghost leads anyone to do LESS.

Under the Law, these property owners would have gotten off easy (speaking in foolish human terms). They would have been expected to tithe, which certainly would not have mandated the sale of property.

Under grace, through the leading of the Holy Spirit dwelling in them, they JOYFULLY sold property and gave all the proceeds to the Apostles. All the Christians' needs were met!

Sadly, in today's Christianity, we cannot say that ALL the needs of the believers are met. Why? Is it because God has failed to provide for His people? **NO! God forbid!**

The reason many saints suffer lack is GREED! Too many of those that God has blessed with wealth hoard it for themselves. Those that are poor have believed the lie that God wants them to keep their money and use it for themselves. This approach is to say that God cannot be trusted, and you need to rely on your resources. It also robs the poor of blessings that God is ready and willing to provide.

The purchase prices were given to the Apostles

Simply amazing! The entire purchase price of the property that was sold was given to the church leadership, the Apostles.

The key in this type of giving must be an attitude of loving obedience to the Holy Spirit. One cannot give like this expecting to obtain something: giving like this will not be blessed of God if done for recognition, status, power, etc.

These Scriptures (Acts chapters 4 and 5) contain an example of properly motivated generosity and an instance of self-motivated generosity. Below we will briefly compare these accounts.

> *"And Joses, who by the apostles was surnamed* ***Barnabas****, (which is, being interpreted, The son of consolation,)* ***a Levite****, and of the country of Cyprus, (37) Having land,* ***sold it, and brought the money, and laid it at the apostles' feet.***" (Acts 4:36-37)

In the passage above, we see that Barnabas owned some property, sold it, and gave it to the Apostles. Barnabas, a Levite, may have been used to receiving tithes as he served the Lord. Here we see how a relationship with Jesus made him selfless and generous.

Barnabas gave generously, and without thinking of himself or what gain he may be able to receive.

On the other hand, there is the account of Ananias and Sapphira in Acts chapter 5. They planned together to make themselves look good by selling property and giving some percentage of it to the Apostles while claiming to have given it all. This example is self-seeking giving, and it is not blessed by God, no matter how much it is worth.

> *"And kept back part of the price, his wife also being privy to it, and brought a certain part, and laid it at the apostles' feet. (3) But Peter said, Ananias, why hath Satan filled thine heart to* **lie to the Holy Ghost**, *and to keep back part of the price of the land?"* (Acts 5:2-3)

The result of this type of lying to God was their destruction.

> *"And Ananias hearing these words* **fell down, and gave up the ghost**: *and great fear came on all them that heard these things."* (Acts 5:5)

Comparing Barnabas with Ananias and Sapphira, we see:

* Both gave generously,
* Barnabas gave out of selfless Holy Spirit-led love,
* Ananias and Sapphira gave out of a desire for fame,
* Barnabas became an apostle,
* Ananias and Sapphira became dead.

The donations were distributed as needed

Initially, the Apostles oversaw the distribution of the donations. There was such abundance that no one suffered lack, and the task of managing the circulation soon became too much for the Apostles. Deacons were appointed to administer these donations.

The bottom line was that no believer suffered any lack. Sadly, we cannot say this in modern Christianity.

Chapter 12 – NT Giving: The Alabaster Box

*"...in the house of **Simon the leper**, as he sat at meat, there came **a woman** having an **alabaster box of ointment** of spikenard **very precious**; and she brake the box, and poured it on his head. (4) And there were some that had indignation within themselves, and said, Why was this waste of the ointment made? (5) **For it might have been sold for more than three hundred pence**, and have been given to the poor. And they murmured..."*
(Mark 14:3-5)

*"Verily I say unto you, **Wheresoever this gospel shall be preached** throughout the whole world, this also that she hath done **shall be spoken of for a memorial of her**. (10) And **Judas Iscariot**, one of the twelve, went unto the chief priests, **to betray him unto them**."* (Mark 14:9-10)

While this account is not directly related to giving in the sense of supporting ministries, it is reflective of New Testament generosity and contrasts it with certain notions.

Many people today champion the idea that the rich should give, and the poor should take; however, is this Biblical? This sounds more like some modern political ideologies than it does Scripture. There are no examples in the pages of the Bible where God endorses such a philosophy.

This philosophy betrays a lack of trust in God. Advocates of such teachings don't believe that God is the Provider of all the needs of His people. They instruct the poor to rely on their resources and the resources of the wealthy. Christians should follow the New Testament examples of how God led the poor to give, and then trust Him!

Yes, God does advocate caring for one another. His Word does teach the wealthy should be voluntarily generous. At the same time, the New Testament examples of giving by the poor are examples of extravagant and cheerful giving.

It is fascinating to note that it was during this account that Judas acted upon his betrayal of Jesus. Here are some observations of the circumstances just before Judas decided to turn on Jesus:

* Jesus was eating in the house of Simon, the leper,
* A woman came and broke an alabaster box and poured the ointment on Jesus,
* Some complained of the waste and said it could have served the poor,
* Jesus defended the woman and proclaimed her fame throughout history.

While we may not know everything going on in the heart of Judas, it is certainly interesting that in the midst of extravagantly generous blessing to Jesus, Judas turned on him. Was it the fact that he held the money bag, and was stealing from it? Was it the fact that Jesus continued to be with the "undesirables" of society? Was it because Jesus' way of doing things did not line up with the way Judas thought they should be done? We don't really know. But we do know that Judas betrayed Jesus amid abundant generosity towards Him.

Chapter 13 – NT Giving: Zacchaeus

> *"And Zacchaeus stood, and said unto the Lord: Behold, Lord, the **half of my goods I give to the poor**; and if I have taken any thing from any man by false accusation, **I restore him fourfold**. (9) And Jesus said unto him, **This day is salvation come to this house**, forsomuch as he also is a son of Abraham."* (Luke 19:8-9)

In this account, we see salvation coming into the life of a tax-collecting liar and thief. Praise Jesus, Who radically changes the lives of people!

Observations from Zacchaeus:

* He promised to give half of his wealth to the poor,
* He promised to pay back four times any thievery,
* Jesus acknowledged Zacchaeus' salvation.

He promised to give half of his wealth to the poor.

Generosity is a true testimony of salvation, especially when the charity is from someone who was previously selfish. Jesus changed Zacchaeus' life, and the change was evidenced in generosity!

Holy Spirit-led giving, in this case, equated to 50% of Zacchaeus' wealth. This passage of Scripture is yet another example of the fact that Christians should never think in terms of tithing only. Giving only "tithes" would be to **LOWER** the standards of the Holy Ghost-led giving.

He promised to pay back four times any thievery.

Not only did Zacchaeus promise generosity going forward. He was led to correct his past thievery and to repay generously what he had stolen. He vowed to pay back four times the amount taken. The Holy Spirit always leads people to excessive generosity.

Jesus acknowledged Zacchaeus' salvation.

Because of Zacchaeus' testimony, Jesus acknowledged that salvation had come to Zacchaeus' home that day.

We have also seen this testimony repeated in the generosity of the Apostle Paul concerning the Corinthians (see 2 Corinthians 9:13).

Compare Zacchaeus with the Rich Young Ruler

> *"Jesus said unto him, If thou wilt be perfect, **go and sell that thou hast, and give to the poor**, and thou shalt have treasure in heaven: and come and follow me. (22) But when the young man heard that saying, **he went away sorrowful: for he had great possessions**."* (Matthew 19:21-22)

How does Zacchaeus compare to the rich young ruler?

* Both had been with Jesus,
* Zacchaeus heard Jesus' and repented and was saved,
* Zacchaeus' repentance was evident in his generosity,
* The young ruler heard Jesus' and rejected His salvation.
* The young ruler's sorrow was a result of his greed.

Giving generously definitely **does not** earn a person salvation. However, generosity is a testimony of a person who has received salvation.

Chapter 14 – Additional Examples of NT Giving

"a devout man and one who feared God with all his household, and **gave many alms to the Jewish people** *and prayed to God continually."*
(Acts 10:2 NASB)

There are several general references to generosity in the Scriptures, and this chapter will briefly review some of these passages. The above verse refers to the generosity of the Roman centurion named Cornelius.

Cornelius

As we have seen with Zacchaeus and others, salvation seems to be evidenced in a person's generosity. Zacchaeus promised to give away half of his wealth, and Jesus immediately stated that salvation had come to Zacchaeus' house, because He understood that Zacchaeus believed Him and trusted God.

In the account of Cornelius, we see his generosity acknowledged at the onset of the story. Cornelius was a Roman soldier; therefore, he was an enemy of the people of Israel. Yet he was God-fearing and generous in almsgiving. Acts 10 presents us with the history of Cornelius' salvation and receiving the Holy Spirit.

The documentation of this event begins with a description of Cornelius: devout, God-fearing, generous, and prayed continually. Isn't it interesting that God included generosity alongside devout, God-fearing, and prayerful?

Is it possible that being free from bondage to money is an indicator of a relationship or a desire for a relationship with God?

John the Baptist

> *"And the people asked him, saying, What shall we do then? (11) He answereth and saith unto them, He that hath two coats, **let him impart to him that hath none**; and he that hath meat, **let him do likewise**. (12) Then came also publicans to be baptized, and said unto him, Master, what shall we do? (13) And he said unto them, **Exact no more than that which is appointed you**. (14) And the soldiers likewise demanded of him, saying, And what shall we do? And he said unto them, Do violence to no man, neither accuse any falsely; and **be content with your wages**."* (Luke 3:10-14)

John the Baptist's ministry preceded the Gospel of Jesus Christ; John, the forerunner of the Messiah, was called to prepare the way of the Lord. Since God does not change, we can study John's ministry in the light of the character and nature of God.

It is very interesting to note that generosity and freedom from greed and slavery to money are a part of each response made by John the Baptist in this passage. He told the people that they should give to others if their own needs are met. He told tax collectors to take only what they were supposed to take. He told soldiers to be content with their wages.

Clearly, John the Baptist understood that people's use of their money needed to change, and would change, if they got right with God. They asked what they needed to do, and John answered in financial terms.

Of course, salvation **cannot be bought!** Again, however, a result of true salvation is generosity!

The Centurion With the Dying Slave

> *"When he heard about Jesus, he sent some Jewish elders asking Him to come and save the life of his slave. (4) When they came to Jesus, they earnestly implored Him, saying, "He is worthy for You to grant this to him; (5) for he loves our nation and **it was he who built us our synagogue.**"*
> (Luke 7:3-5 NASB)

Once again, it is fascinating how God deems it essential to include this Roman centurion's generosity in this account. Time and time again, we see throughout the Bible that people in a right relationship with God (or who desire such a relationship) possess the characteristic of generosity!

There are other examples that we could cite, and each is exemplary of real big-heartedness. However, we will conclude this chapter with two verses of Scripture to ponder.

> *"For **where your treasure is**, there will **your heart be also**."* (Matthew 6:21)

> *"It is easier for a camel to go through the eye of a needle, than for a **rich man to enter into the kingdom of God**."* (Mark 10:25)

Chapter 15 – NT Giving: Who Tithed - Who Didn't

As we have seen in the previous chapters, there are many examples of people in the New Testament whose extravagant giving dwarfed the requirements of the Law. In this chapter, we will look at those who tithed and those who did not.

Holy Spirit-led giving, as evidenced throughout the New Testament, is always bountiful giving. But are there any Bible examples of people who only tithed? Are there Bible examples of people who gave less than a tithe? As Christians, the answers to these questions should be relevant to us as we develop our strategies for giving.

Does the Bible have any examples of people who tithed?

Yes, there are a few passages in the New Testament that tell us of people who believed in tithing. Here are a couple of these references:

> *"The **Pharisee** stood and prayed thus with himself, God, I thank thee, that I am not as other men are, extortioners, unjust, adulterers, or even as this publican. (12) I fast twice in the week, **I give tithes of all that I possess**."*
> (Luke 18:11-12)

> *"Woe unto you, **scribes and Pharisees**, hypocrites! for **ye pay tithe** of mint and anise and cummin, and have omitted the weightier matters of the law, judgment, mercy, and faith: **these ought ye to have done**, and not to leave the other undone."*
> (Matthew 23:23)

So we see that the scribes and Pharisees were tithe payers, and we see in the verse above that Jesus expected tithes to continue.

Does the Bible have any examples of people who gave LESS than a tithe?

Biblical examples of people who did not give tithes could not be found while researching this book. Of course, this does not mean that such people did not exist; it merely means that God chose not to mention them in the Scriptures.

New Testament giving examples:

There is a good amount of information in the New Testament regarding Christian giving. Below is an overview of the types of giving that existed in the Bible.

* Give Generously More Than Tithes - Rich and poor alike, the Biblical example is that anyone who honored God gave in abundance.

* Give Tithes - The Bible does provide examples of people who gave only tithes. The self-righteous scribes and Pharisees were tithe payers, and they were proud of it.

* Give Less Than Tithes - The New Testament seems to be silent concerning those who gave less than the Law required. There is assuredly no praise in the Scriptures for those who did not give the minimums of the Law.

* Give Deceptively - The account of Ananias and Sapphira is a sobering reminder that a generous gift from a lying heart incurs harsh punishment.

From the examples available to us in the Word of God, it is clear that Holy Spirit-led giving will be very generous. It will always be extravagant when compared to the requirements of the Law.

Chapter 16 – Instructions – Paid Ministry

Temple Priests and Gospel Preachers

In today's Christianity, there is a mistaken notion that there is no valid comparison between the priests of the Old Testament Temple and New Testament preachers of the Gospel. In efforts to dismiss tithing, believers attempt to divorce any association between these two ministers of God. This "separation" is artificial and is in opposition to the teaching of the Bible.

While it is true that little is stated explicitly with regards to tithing in the New Testament (although Jesus did address it), there is much said in the realms of money and stewardship. The purposes and principles of tithing in the Old Testament have not changed in the New Testament; therefore, our handling of God's money continues to be very important. We must be involved in fulfilling God's plans for the money (and other things) that He gives us stewardship over.

In any case, Paul draws an obvious parallel between the preachers of the Gospel and priests of the Temple. Much of 1 Corinthians chapter 9 discusses the suitability of God's people providing for the needs of God's ministers.

> *"Do ye not know that they which minister about holy things live of the things of the temple? and they which wait at the altar are partakers with the altar? (14)* **Even so hath the Lord ordained that they which preach the gospel should live of the gospel."** (1 Corinthians 9:13-14)

It is essential to note the following from 1 Corinthians 9:13-14:

* The priests of the Temple made their living from their ministry unto God,
* God has ordained that Gospel preachers should be paid,
* Preachers of the Gospel ought to make their living from the preaching of the Gospel.

Paul asks, "**Don't you know** that ministers of the Temple make their living from their ministry?" Paul expects them to have complete knowledge of the fact that the Temple priests were provided for by the tithes as the reward for their ministry. Many of these believers in Corinth would have been Gentiles and may not have been aware of God's plans to provide for His ministers; therefore, **Paul is teaching them the Law of Moses and applying the principles of it to those who preach the Gospel**.

There is also an exciting fact here that might be easily overlooked. This detail is found in the English two-letter word "so" near the beginning of verse 14.

We can look at this word and think of it simply as a comparative connection between Old Testament priests and New Testament Gospel preachers; however, it may be more than that. The Greek word means "in this manner" or "in this way" ("houtō(s)" - Strong's G3779).

This passage is saying, "The way that the priests of the Temple made their living from the work of their ministry, in the same way, Gospel preachers ought to make their living." In light of this, we must ask:

Question: How did the priests make their living?

Answer: Primarily from the TITHES!

> *"And, behold, **I have given the children of Levi all the tenth in Israel** for an inheritance, **for their service which they serve**, even the service of the tabernacle of the congregation."* (Numbers 18:21)

In the Old Covenant, the Law demanded that tithes be given to meet the needs of the priests. Under the New Covenant, Christians are led by the Holy Spirit to give tithes and **more** to provide for God's ministers (as well as the needy.)

Under the Old Covenant, God mandated this provision because He knew the hearts of the people and that His priests would not receive the necessary care. Under the New Covenant, He has given His people new hearts, hearts that God should be able to trust to do right and provide for His ministers.

Under the Old Covenant, works of the flesh and obedience to the Law supplied the needs of God's ministers. In the New Covenant, the Holy Ghost empowers God's people to give and support His ministers.

Is it even possible to consider that Christians, under the grace of God in the infinitely superior New Covenant, could feasibly be led by the Holy Spirit to do LESS than the minimum requirement of the Law? This is completely unimaginable!

Example of Paid Ministries – The Apostles

> *"Do we not have the right to take along a believing wife, as do the other apostles and the brothers of the Lord and Cephas? (6) Or is it only Barnabas*

*and I **who have no right to refrain from working for a living?"** (1 Corinthians 9:5-6 ESV)

The Holy Spirit writes through the Apostle Paul that the other apostles, including Peter, and the brothers of Jesus were involved in full-time paid ministry. They were exercising their *"right to refrain from working for a living."* This passage is referring to working a secular job on top of fulfilling the ministry work to which God had called them.

Paul inquires if it just he and Barnabas who did not have this right to earn their living from their ministry of the Gospel. Thus Paul teaches that Gospel preachers ought to be able to make their living from the Gospel, as the Lord commanded. (see 1 Corinthians 9:13-14 referenced above)

Interestingly, Paul himself chooses NOT to exercise this right.

> *"But I have made no use of any of these **rights**, nor am I writing these things to secure any such provision. For I would rather die than have anyone deprive me of my ground for boasting.*
> (1 Corinthians 9:15 - ESV)

Does Paul's personal choice not to use these **rights**, **negate** or **invalidate** the doctrines that he just taught? Paul taught and acknowledged his **right** to paid ministry, but chose not to use that right.

If you have the **right** to vote, but you choose not to vote, does that mean that your **right** to vote no longer exists?

Example of Paid Ministries – Jesus' Disciples

*"And **commanded** them that they should take nothing for their journey, save a staff only; no scrip, no bread, **no money in their purse**:"* (Mark 6:8)

*"And if the son of peace be there, your peace shall rest upon it: if not, it shall turn to you again. (7) And in the same house remain, eating and drinking such things as they give: for the **labourer is worthy of his hire**. Go not from house to house."*
(Luke 10:6-7)

When Jesus commissioned His disciples during His earthly ministry, He told them **not** to take any money and to find their provision in the households of believers in each location where they preached. Jesus taught that the **worker is worthy of his wages**.

Sadly, many Christian leaders abuse this doctrine and manipulate other believers based upon these concepts; however, abuses of **truth** never invalidate the **truth**.

The **truth** is that God **loves** and **cares** for His servants, and He has set up parameters and guidelines for their provisions. God has **ordained** that His legitimate ministers should be provided for by His legitimate children.

Chapter 17 – Instructions – Share All Good Things

> *"The one who is taught the word is to share all good things with the one who teaches him. (7) Do not be deceived, **God is not mocked**; for whatever a man sows, this he will also reap. (8) For the one who sows to his own flesh will from the flesh reap corruption, but the one who sows to the Spirit will from the Spirit reap eternal life. (9) Let us not lose heart in doing good, for in due time we will reap if we do not grow weary. (10) So then, while we have opportunity, let us do good to all people, and especially to those who are of the household of the faith."* (Galatians 6:6-10 NASB)

This passage contains several different aspects of Christian giving instructions. It speaks of three levels of giving, what to give, and what not to give, encouragement towards giving, etc.

Three Levels of Giving

Giving to your Teachers - Paul instructs the student to "share all good things" with the teacher. What does this mean? The Greek word translated *share* in this passage is very informative and adds a depth of understanding to what is being said. It is the word "koinōneō" (see Strong's G2841), and it is defined as:

"to come into communion or fellowship with, to become a sharer, be made a partner - to enter into fellowship, join one's self to an associate, make one's self a sharer or partner"

As we can see, this Greek word goes far beyond merely giving to our spiritual teachers. We should literally become a partner with our instructors in Christ. We should share in their ministry, and as we grow, we will even share their ministry. We will often repeat to others lessons we have learned from those who taught us.

Giving to fellow Christians - Paul teaches that our good works (i.e., "doing good") should next focus on our brothers and sisters in Christ. After we have shared "all good things" with our spiritual educators, next, we focus on those in the "household of faith." That is, if we see another believer in need, we should reach out to them in the love of Jesus and attempt to meet their need.

Giving to all - Paul teaches that when we have the opportunity, we should be generous unto all people.

These instructions should be helpful in our decisions regarding our giving. It should sadden all believers to see older Christian leaders, who are often lonely and uncared for, after they have worked lifetimes to teach and impart the Word of God to people. It should also be disheartening to see full-time ministers who are diligently serving their community but still need to work second and third jobs to provide for their families.

Paul tells Timothy that good elders who work in the Word of God and doctrine are worthy of double honor.

> *"Let the elders that rule well be counted **worthy of double honour, especially they who labour in the word and doctrine.**"* (1 Timothy 5:17)

This "double honor" idea aligns itself well with the principle of "sharing all good things" with your teachers. It is also fascinating to do a word study on what "double honor" means. The Greek words that God chose to use in this verse provide some powerful insights. Here are the Greek words:

of double = Strong's G1362 – "diplous – twofold, double"

honor = Strong's G5092 – "timē – a valuing by which the price is fixed - of the price itself - of the price paid or received for a person or thing bought or sold - honour which belongs or is shown to one - of the honour which one has by reason of rank and state of office which he holds - deference, reverence"

Isn't it interesting that the Greek word for *honor* has a monetary aspect as part of its definition? It also includes respect for the position.

Therefore, good elders are worthy of twice as much respect and monetary value. This book will not attempt to put a dollar amount on this value; however, it should be noted that good elders should not be taken for granted and undervalued.

All Good Things

This passage tells us that we are supposed to share "all good things" with those who teach us. If that person is an elder laboring in the Word of God and doctrine, they are worthy of double honor, and that definition includes finances. So what does the phrase "all good things" mean?

good things = Strong's G18 – "agathos – of good constitution or nature - useful, salutary - good, pleasant, agreeable, joyful, happy - excellent, distinguished - upright, honourable"

As we can see by the word God chose to use, we are to share all useful, pleasant, joyful, honorable, upright, and marvelous things with those who teach us. Taking the double honor passage into consideration, sharing our financial blessings are certainly included.

This way of thinking is reflective of an *attitude of gratitude*. How thankful are you to those who teach you the Word of God? Especially with regards to those who God used to lead you to Jesus!

Don't Be Deceived – God Isn't Mocked!

> *"Do not be deceived, **God is not mocked**; for whatever a man sows, this he will also reap."*
> (Galatians 6:7)

Isn't it interesting that immediately following Paul's instruction to share all good things with your spiritual teachers, God warns us not to be deceived and tells us He is not mocked!

It seems that Paul is associating *taking for granted your spiritual instructors* with *mocking Him*! Surely if we take a deep breath and ponder this thought, it makes sense.

God sent and ordained our spiritual mentors. He called them to help us grow in the faith. They are commissioned to assist us in becoming spiritually mature. If we do not look after them, are we not indeed mocking God?

Sowing And Reaping

Paul clarifies his doctrine even more. He follows his statement about God not being mocked with a discussion of sowing and reaping. These remarks are specifically in the context of caring for our teachers in Christ. Cross-referencing this passage with another from Paul shows us clearly the connection to monetary giving.

> *"But this I say, He which **soweth sparingly shall reap also sparingly**; and he which **soweth bountifully shall reap also bountifully**. (7) Every man according as **he purposeth in his heart, so let him give**; not grudgingly, or of necessity: for God loveth a cheerful giver."* (2 Corinthians 9:6-7)

Almost all Christians know about verse 7, that we are supposed to give cheerfully as we purpose in our hearts. Sadly, few are aware of the context of sowing and reaping in verse 6. If one takes verses 6 and 7 in context (along with the rest of the chapter), there is no legitimate reason to make allowance for minimal giving.

In our passage from Galatians (quoted above), we see Paul comparing sowing "to the flesh" or "to the Spirit." In context, sowing to the flesh would be spending "all good things" on yourself, while sowing to the Spirit is equated with "sharing all good things" with your spiritual mentors. Sowing to the flesh reaps a harvest of corruption, and sowing to the Spirit reaps eternal life.

The Apostle Paul's explicit instructions are for believers to share generously in all good things with their spiritual leaders. It is such a serious consideration that the Holy Spirit, through Paul, associates a lack of care for spiritual instructors with mocking God and leading to corruption.

Chapter 18 – Instructions – Systematic Giving

*"Now **concerning the collection for the saints**, as I directed the churches of Galatia, so do you also. (2) On the first day of every week each one of you is to put aside and save, as he may prosper, so that no collections be made when I come."*
(1 Corinthians 16:1-2 NASB)

We see in these verses, the Apostle Paul teaching a systematic approach to giving. To avoid rushed and minimized collections upon Paul's arrival, he gives direction with regards to collecting offerings for the saints.

This collection was intended for the persecuted saints in Jerusalem (see 1 Corinthians 16:3). There is an expectation from Paul that the Corinthians would give generously each week.

Below are some insights to be gained from this passage.

Observations from these verses:

* Collection for the saints,
* Paul directed the churches giving practices,
* The first day of every week,
* Every person,
* Set aside and save,
* As the Lord prospers,
* To avoid collections when Paul arrived.

Collection for the saints

This passage speaks of collections for the saints to be sent to the persecuted church in Jerusalem. Paul is receiving this collection from the church at Corinth as well as the churches in Galatia. Therefore, he is passing on the same instructions.

Paul directed the churches giving practices

This portion of verse 1 is very interesting. In the quoted New American Standard Bible (NASB), Paul writes, "...as I **directed** the churches of Galatia..." other translations use the word **order** instead. The King James Version says, "…as I have given **order**…"

Many state that the Bible advocates free-will giving. If by this one means Spirit-led free-will giving, then that is an accurate portrayal of the Biblical pattern. The orders Paul gives to the churches of Corinth, and Galatia fall into the Holy Spirit-led giving models.

So what does this word **directed** mean? The Greek word translated "directed" is the word *diatassō,* and it means "to arrange, appoint, ordain, prescribe, give order."

This word is used seventeen times in the New Testament, and seven of these are translated as "**command**" in the King James Version. Other English words used are "appoint," "ordain," "set in order," etc.

Suffice it to say; this passage does not appear to be a just good idea. It is the Apostle Paul giving clear directives about the collection for the saints.

The first day of every week

In verse 2, we see Paul detailing his instructions for giving. The first step in Paul's systematic pattern of giving is that they should establish a model of preparing their offerings on the first day of every week. Developing a consistent system is critical to fruitful and faithful giving.

Every person

Paul's second step in this offering preparation is that every person should participate. Everyone who has experienced the Lord's provision was instructed to participate in this systematic collection.

Set aside and save

The third step in Paul's systematic giving instructions is to purposely put aside money every week and accumulate it and store it for the time of the offering. Paul understood the power of money, so he is establishing a systematic approach to giving that will make the process more effective.

Think about it this way. If you give $50 per week in charitable giving, that is $2,600 per year. Is it easier to give the $50 each week or $2,600 once per year? Even though the amount is the same, most would have much greater difficulty writing one check for the annualized amount.

Paul's teaching about systematic giving is efficient and will help each one to be faithful to the Lord. It is also patterned after the methods and principles God established in the Old Testament.

As the Lord prospers us

The fourth step of Paul's instructions is that each person should accumulate every week, according to the Lord's provision. Again, Paul is well acquainted with the faithfulness of God, and the expectation is that each person will experience God's provision and therefore be givers. Paul knew that God's provision was in accord with God's riches in glory and that the Christian response should be that of generosity.

The concept of giving based upon the Lord's provision goes back to the Old Testament. The first indication of bringing the best of the Lord's provision to God can be seen in the offerings of Cain and Abel. Both offered to God from the increase of His provision, but Abel offered the best, while Cain offered a lesser gift.
(See Genesis 4:3-4)

This concept of giving based upon God's provision is also seen in the Law regarding tithing.

> *"Thou shalt truly **tithe all the increase** of thy seed, that the field bringeth forth year by year."*
> (Deuteronomy 14:22)

It is not surprising that an all-knowing and perfect God who is the same forever would not change his principles of giving from the Old Testament to the New Testament. The principles remain the same; what has changed is the indwelling of the Holy Spirit. Our willingness and ability to give cheerfully and generously comes from Christ in us.

To avoid collections when Paul arrived

The final step of Paul's teaching about systematic giving is that it should not be on the spur of the moment. Paul did not want a frantic collection to be made upon his arrival. Paul knew that the offering and relief that it would bring would be far more significant with a systematic giving process compared to a collection blitz after Paul arrived.

For example, assume that you had to buy your next vehicle with cash. Which approach would allow you to obtain a better vehicle?

* Save $250 per month for five years towards a purchase,
* Wait until your current vehicle is no longer functional.

Most people would be better equipped for a vehicle purchase if they took the systematic savings approach. Paul is applying this same principle in these instructions.

Summary

The Apostle Paul gives scripturally based orders (i.e., directions) for the establishment of systematic giving, to develop an effective method for generous giving.

Chapter 19 – Instructions – The Rich and Giving

> *"Instruct those who are rich in this present world* ***not to be conceited*** *or to fix their* **hope** *on the uncertainty of riches, but* **on God***, who richly supplies us with all things to enjoy. (18) Instruct them to* **do good***, to* **be rich in good works***, to* **be generous** *and* **ready to share***, (19)* ***storing up for themselves the treasure*** *of a good foundation for the future, so that they may* **take hold of that which is life indeed***."* (1 Timothy 6:17-19 NASB)

This chapter will review some of the instructions that the Apostle Paul gives to Timothy to pass on to wealthy Christians. Many will read this chapter with satisfaction that the rich are being instructed in generous giving, and it is true. However, we must keep in mind that all of us (rich and poor alike) need to place our confidence in God for our provision. If God is the source for all of our needs, does it not make sense that all of us should be generous, as the Lord prospers us?

Observations from Paul's instructions to the wealthy:

* Don't be conceited or trust in riches,
* Trust in God Who supplies all things to enjoy,
* Do good,
* Be rich in good works,
* Be generous,
* Be ready to share,
* Store up the treasure of a good foundation for the future,
* To take hold of real life.

Below we will briefly examine each of these points of instruction from Paul.

Don't be conceited or trust in riches

Humanity has not changed. Like today, Paul was aware that the wealthy could have a tendency to trust in their wealth, and think highly of themselves for their accomplishments. The Apostle Paul warns against such vain reliance upon wealth. Paul echoes the thoughts of Jesus, who said in the parable about the rich man who built bigger barns:

> *"But God said unto him,* **Thou fool***, this night thy soul shall be required of thee: then whose shall those things be, which thou hast provided?"* (Luke 12:20)

Trust in God Who supplies all things to enjoy

The next aspect of Paul's instructions reveals two important things. First, he teaches that the wealthy should trust God instead of their riches. Trusting God is good advice for everyone, but the wealthy often can trust in their assets more quickly than the poor. The second item to take note of is that God gives all things to enjoy.

Often, we view God as a very serious and somber kill-joy. Nothing could be further from the truth! God wants us to enjoy life and bestows many blessings on us to accomplish this enjoyment. The beauty of this is that what God provides is what is truly necessary for a fulfilled life.

If we are faithful in our stewardship over what God has entrusted to us, He will make sure we have what we need to lead a contented and satisfying life. Here is what He tells us:

"And God is able to make all grace abound toward you; that ye, always having all sufficiency in all things, may abound to every good work:"
(2 Corinthians 9:8)

Do good

To "do good" might seem to be a generic encouragement; however, checking the Greek word used in this case adds a bit more insight. It is the Greek word "agathoergeō" (Strong's G14), and it means "to work good, to do good, to do well, act rightly."

Paul is instructing the affluent Christians to be good workers and to behave properly. They should not use their wealth as a tool to allow for improper or lazy behavior.

Be rich in good works

Being rich in good works is also more clearly understood with a brief look at the Greek words. Being rich in this case is the word "plouteō" (Strong's G4147), and it means "to be rich, to have abundance - is affluent in resources so that he can give blessings…to all."

In this case, Paul is calling the wealthy to abound in ministering to the needs of all, from the riches of the blessings of God's provisions. They should overflow with good works.

The Greek word for works is "ergon" (Strong's G2041). The meaning of this word includes: "business, employment, that with which any one is occupied - that which one undertakes to do, enterprise, undertaking - any product whatever, any thing accomplished by hand, art, industry, or mind."

Thus we see that Paul wants the well-off Christians to make it their business to be bountiful in producing many works that bless others, above and beyond their financial giving.

Be generous

Paul describes the liberality with which those who are wealthy should give. They should be generous.

Be ready to share

In Greek, this phrase embodies fellowship and communion. It is reflective of the desired attitude of the affluent Christians. Fundamentally, these believers should want to make others share in their blessings. Along with being generous, they should do so freely and willingly.

Store up the treasure of a good foundation for the future, to take hold of real life.

There is a saying in some Christian circles that goes like this: "You can't take it with you, but you can send it on ahead."

This saying is substantially supported by the following Scripture (1 Corinthians 3:12). By adhering to Paul's instructions in Christ, the wealthy can build with gold, silver, and precious stones, instead of building with wood, hay, and stubble.

> *"Now if any man build upon this foundation gold, silver, precious stones, wood, hay, stubble;"*
> (1 Corinthians 3:12)

Chapter 20 – Instructions – Render To Caesar

"They say unto him, Caesar's. Then saith he unto them, Render therefore unto Caesar the things which are Caesar's; and unto God the things that are God's." (Matthew 22:21)

In this passage, the religious leaders attempted to trick Jesus with a question that they thought He could not answer. They asked Jesus if it was lawful to pay tribute to Caesar.

If Jesus had simply answered "Yes," there could be some laws and promises from God, which Jesus could have violated.

If Jesus had simply answered "No," He would have condoned violating Roman law.

Instead, Jesus answered in a way that directed the question towards spiritual truths. Give to Caesar what is his, and give to God what is His.

Therefore, the real question here is, "What belongs to God?"

The first verses that we want to look at are:

*"And all the **tithe of the land**, whether of the seed of the land, or of the fruit of the tree, is the Lord's: **it is holy unto the Lord**."* (Leviticus 27:30)

*"And concerning the **tithe of the herd**, or of the flock, even of whatsoever passeth under the rod, the **tenth shall be holy unto the Lord**."*

(Leviticus 27:32)

Here we can see that the tithes were holy unto the Lord. So, can something that God calls holy be unholy? If God says that tithes are holy unto Himself, does the Bible teach that tithes have become unholy or unnecessary?

Here is something else from Scripture that tells us what belongs to God:

> *"The **earth is the Lord's**, and the fulness thereof; the world, and they that dwell therein."*
> (Psalm 24:1)

God's ownership of everything falls nicely in line with the extravagant Spirit-led giving that we see in the New Testament. Recall the previous chapters in this book, which detail the type of giving that pleases God. New Testament believers gave as though they **really believed** that the earth is the Lord's!

Thus the reality of giving to God what belongs to Him is that we give Him everything. He says that the tithes are holy unto the Lord, giving this minimum requirement of the Law that God gave to Moses is a beginning. It says, *"I trust you, Lord, you own everything, and you will take care of me."*

Chapter 21 – The First Money Problems in the Church

> *"Now in these days when the disciples were increasing in number, a complaint by the Hellenists arose against the Hebrews because their widows were being neglected in the daily distribution."*
> (Acts 6:1 - ESV)

Not surprising, the very first recorded problem in the Bible, after the establishment of the church on the day of Pentecost, involved money. We see in the above verse that the Hellenistic believers complained that they were unfairly treated in the daily distributions of wealth. These distributions were likely in the form of food.

Read the end of Acts chapter four, and you will see that great resources were being donated to the ministry of the church in Jerusalem. The disposition of these resources was discussed in a previous chapter; however, in summary, anyone who held land or houses sold them and gave the sale price to the Apostles. The Apostles, in turn, distributed the resources as needed, and no believer suffered any lack.

Before the daily distribution problem (noted above), we have the account of Ananias and Sapphira in Acts chapter five. In this case, they sought recognition as having sold land and given the entire price to the Apostles; however, they lied about the value and kept some for themselves. As you will recall, they were struck dead for lying to the Holy Ghost.

The first problem within the church *body* is found in Acts chapter six, when the complaint about inequitable distributions of these resources, quickly arose.

While this, of course, has no direct bearing on tithing or giving, it does demonstrate the power of money to cause problems. These two examples reveal the early stages of financial troubles within the body of Christ. As we review history since the time of the early church, we can see a digression from:

...No Christian suffered any lack...

...To today, where many suffer severe lack...

It appears that we desperately need to get back to the New Testament patterns of giving and trusting in the Lord.

Chapter 22 – Problem – The Love Of Money

*"For the **love of money is the root of all evil**: which while some **coveted after**, they **have erred from the faith**, and pierced themselves through with many sorrows."* (1 Timothy 6:10)

Many problems can be associated with money. This verse tells us that the "love of money" is the root of all evil! Since this book is about tithing and New Testament giving, it is relevant to understand something of the evils that may result from the existence, use, and abuse of money in ministry.

As we noted in the previous chapter, money was at the root of the first recorded problems of the church, which was birthed at Pentecost. Ananias and Sapphira were struck dead because of the love of money; and the perceived inequities of the daily distributions sparked the first controversy in the body of believers. In these examples alone, we can see the truth of 1 Timothy 6:10.

The LOVE of money:

The problem is not directly with money itself, but rather with the love of money. The poor and rich alike can suffer the maladies of the love of wealth.

It is a flawed concept to think that those in poverty cannot be afflicted with the love of money. A simple reading of the newspaper or watching the news on television demonstrates this notion to be flawed. Every day poor people with a love of money commit crimes to get more money.

It is equally wrong to think that the wealthy are immune to the love of money. The possession of money creates the allure to obtain more money. Obsession with investing, growing business, earning more, can easily overcome those of affluence. Similar to those in poverty, every day some rich people commit crimes to gain more money.

In the church, the "love of money" often manifests itself in particularly ugly ways. It should also be noted that when Christians abuse money, the world is watching more closely. We must always be vigilant to avoid doing anything to cause God's work to be discredited.

> "Giving no offence in any thing, that the ministry be not blamed:" (2 Corinthians 6:3)

Of the plethora of books available today that claim to be about tithing, many are, in fact, responses to the abuses by many churches, pastors, and religious leaders. The Bible is filled with instructions for Christians about giving, and these instructions can indeed be manipulated to fleece the sheep.

The problem here is that most of these books mix two issues and treat them as one. Here are the two issues: first, what do the Scriptures teach about New Testament giving; second, how are we supposed to address the abuses of people and their money that are evident in the body of Christ?

By confusing these two issues into one, many tithing books and teachings arrive at the simple conclusion of give as you purpose in your heart. Today, this often equates to giving little or nothing, so there are obvious problems with such out-of-context over-simplification. Please refer back to chapter three of this book for a detailed analysis of this concept.

Generally, many simplify the idea of giving as you purpose in your heart to the notion of free-will giving, as follows:

Free-will giving means that I am free to give what I want, but I am also free not to give.

Spirit-led giving means that I am free to obey the Holy Spirit, or I am free to disobey the Holy Spirit.

As you can see, there is a HUGE DIFFERENCE between free-will giving (i.e., without the Holy Spirit's guidance) and Holy Spirit-led giving.

Erred from the faith:

Loving money can cause severe problems. Coveting money may lead to erring from the faith. So, what does it mean to err from the faith? The Greek word translated "they have erred" is the word "apoplanaō" (Strong's G635), and it means:

"to cause to go astray - to lead away from the truth to error - to go astray, stray away from."

Leaving the truth to embrace error is not a good thing. Going astray takes us away from the Lord, and results in many sorrows.

The love of money combined with the idea of free-will giving (severed from the leading of the Holy Spirit) leads to what is too often evident in Christianity today, that is, GREED and minimal, if any, giving. Some polls have shown that less than 10% of Christians give tithes or more.

If such surveys were taken at the birth of the church immediately following Pentecost, they would have different results. According to what is recorded in the Bible, you would have been hard-pressed to find anyone who gave less than a tenth.

The body of Christ needs to lose its love of money and return to Spirit-led giving!

Chapter 23 – Tithes And Circumcision

Some Christians, who oppose the idea that tithing is a practice that should be continued under grace, compare the giving of tithes to circumcision. They note that circumcision is no longer mandated under grace; therefore, tithing is similarly no longer required. There are some problems with this notion; we will review three of them in this chapter.

First - Circumcision was a SIGN of God's Covenant with Abraham:

> *"And God said unto Abraham, Thou shalt keep my covenant therefore, thou, and thy seed after thee in their generations. (10) This is my covenant, which ye shall keep, between me and you and thy seed after thee; Every man child among you shall be circumcised. (11) And ye shall circumcise the flesh of your foreskin;* **and it shall be a token of the covenant betwixt me and you**.*"* (Genesis 17:9-11)

The first time in the Bible that we learn of circumcision, we see that it is symbolic of God's covenant with Abraham. This symbol pre-dates the Law and represents the covenant promise and relationship between God and Abraham. This emblem was a token of the promise of God to Abraham at the onset of the Old Covenant.

Tithing, like circumcision, also pre-dates the Law. However, the purpose of tithing was never **symbolic** of God's covenant, certainly not the Old Covenant. If anything, tithing is associated with the New Covenant! The first mention of tithing in the Bible is in regards to Melchisedec. Jesus, the fulfillment of the New Covenant, is a Priest forever after the order of Melchisedec. Therefore, tithing is associated with the Priestly Order of the New Covenant. (Review the other chapters related to Melchisedec and tithing pre-dating the Law for additional information.)

Second - Both Testaments clarify that God's desired Circumcision was not of the flesh but the heart:

> *"Circumcise yourselves to the LORD, and take away the **foreskins of your heart**, ye men of Judah and inhabitants of Jerusalem: lest my fury come forth like fire, and burn that none can quench it, because of the evil of your doings."* (Jeremiah 4:4)

> *"But he is a Jew, which is one inwardly; and **circumcision is that of the heart**, in the spirit, and not in the letter; whose praise is not of men, but of God."* (Romans 2:29)

Unlike circumcision, the tithe serves **external** (physical) purposes. Circumcision is one of the descriptions of how God deals with our hearts. True circumcision deals with the **internal** purposes of God (purity of heart).

The purposes of tithing are primarily external, and these same purposes continue today. You may recall from previous chapters that some of these include: providing for God's ministers; providing for the poor and widows; and expressions of thankfulness unto God.

The Bible never clarifies tithing as being a spiritual or internal teaching, whereas, by comparison, both testaments make it clear that the circumcision God requires is that of the heart.

Note: tithing does reveal the internal or spiritual realities of what is in a person's heart; however, God's stated purposes for giving are primarily provisional and physically focused.

Tithing was implemented by God to meet practical physical needs. Circumcision was implemented by God to symbolize His provision for eternal spiritual needs. A comparison of tithing with circumcision to dismiss tithing is a flawed analogy.

Third - Jesus is the Fulfillment of God's Promise to Abraham:

This is likely the most potent reason that circumcision of the flesh is no longer a mandate. God promised Abraham blessings through his seed, and the Apostle Paul clarifies that Jesus is that Seed.

> *"Now to Abraham and his seed were the promises made. He saith not, And to seeds, as of many; but as of one, **And to thy seed, which is Christ**."*
> (Galatians 3:16)

> *"And if ye be Christ's, then are ye Abraham's seed, and heirs according to the promise."*
> (Galatians 3:29)

Therefore, the promise which circumcision symbolized has been fulfilled. It makes no sense to keep a token of a promise that is no longer **symbolic** but has already become a fulfilled **reality**.

The coming of Jesus has not removed the need of God's ministers for provision. The Messiah's arrival has not yet eradicated poverty. Jesus' coming has not eliminated the proper expression of thankfulness demonstrated by giving to God. The needs that God addressed through tithing all continue to exist.

Summary of Major Differences:

As you can see, comparing tithing with circumcision in order to disassociate tithing from the New Covenant is a flawed approach.

* Circumcision is a symbol of the covenant between God and Abraham,
* tithing is an actual method by which God provides for physical needs,
* circumcision was a symbol of the Old Covenant,
* tithing first shows up in the Bible with regard to Melchisedec, a New Covenant representative,
* the promise that circumcision symbolized has been fulfilled in Jesus,
* the needs that tithes were ordained to meet continue to exist today.

Chapter 24 – Tithes and the Sabbath

Some Christians compare the giving of tithes to keeping the Sabbath. They note that most Christians no longer worship on Saturday and thus seem to be free from the Law of keeping the Sabbath. Problems with comparing tithing to the keeping of the Sabbath will be discussed in this chapter.

First - The Sabbath was designed to be a day of rest:

> *"And he said unto them, This is that which the LORD hath said, To morrow is **the rest of the holy sabbath** unto the LORD: bake that which ye will bake to day, and seethe that ye will seethe; and that which remaineth over lay up for you to be kept until the morning."* (Exodus 16:23)

The passage above from Exodus 16 is the first time the word *Sabbath* is used in the Bible. It is referring to the seventh day of Creation, which God both designated as a day of rest and sanctified. During their time of wandering in the desert, God directed the children of Israel to gather enough manna for today and tomorrow (Exodus 16:5) and to do today whatever meal preparations were necessary, so that they could then rest on the Sabbath.

Like tithing and circumcision, the Sabbath also pre-dates the Law. The purpose of the Sabbath was to set an example for people to rest. God Himself certainly did not need to rest; however, He knew that we would need rest.

Like tithing, the Sabbath was designed to meet physical needs: A person who observes the Sabbath obtains rest for themselves; a person, who tithes, provides for the needs of others.

Second - Jesus clarified the point that the Sabbath was for a person's benefit:

> *"And he said unto them, The **sabbath was made for man**, and not man for the sabbath:"* (Mark 2:27)

> *"For the Son of man is Lord even of the sabbath day."* (Matthew 12:8)

Jesus makes it clear that the Sabbath was made for man. Jesus freed people from slavery to laws, interpreted by people, by returning to the original intention of the Sabbath day. It is God's example to people that we need rest. We are **FREE to rest** (and we should)! We are **NOT ENSLAVED** to a particular day.

Jesus never clarified tithing in any similar manner. The Sabbath is for the benefit of the individual observing it, whereas the tithe is for the benefit of the recipient.

Major Differences and Chapter Summary:

Since there are significant differences between tithing and keeping the Sabbath, any comparisons designed to invalidate tithing are taken out of context.

* **Sabbaths benefit the person observing it**. It is a day of rest for them.

* **Tithes benefit the person receiving the tithe**. It is a provision of God for them.

* **Sabbath Laws were clarified and defined** by Jesus and Paul in the way God intended.

* Tithe Laws had no additional clarification necessary. The purpose of the tithe has not changed.

Similar to comparisons with circumcision, reviewing tithing in the light of Sabbath days is a wrong approach. A better comparison would be to compare tithing laws to other moral laws such as "Honor your father and mother" or "Thou shalt not kill." God expects and empowers us to keep these moral laws.

Attempts to use Sabbath laws to invalidate the practices of tithing (or better yet, Holy Spirit-led giving) reflect a misunderstanding of the Bible. This type of teaching leads to a lack of provision in the body of Christ.

Chapter 25 – The Purposes of Tithes

This chapter will compare the reasons given by God for tithing in the Old Testament with what the New Testament has to say about giving. It should teach us a great deal about God and our Christian giving.

God has not ever changed (that is what He says of Himself). His immutability being true, then it is reasonable to deduce that His reasons for tithing and giving should be very similar in both Testaments. If the purposes are the same, then it is unlikely that the mode of giving would have changed.

> *"For **I am the LORD, I change not**; therefore ye sons of Jacob are not consumed."* (Malachi 3:6)

It is fascinating to note that one of the verses in which God clearly states that He does not change is in the immediate context of the tithe. Is it possible God knew that His people would attempt to justify their lack of giving by rejecting the teaching of the tithe? First, we see Malachi 3:6 quoted above; then two verses later (verse 8), we see God rebuking His people for robbing Him concerning tithing.

The Old Testament Reasons for Tithing

Melchisedec is discussed in some detail in another chapter of this book. However, since the following reference is the first mention of tithing in the Bible, we must touch on it briefly here.

OT Reason: Gratitude for blessings received from the minister of God.

In Genesis 14:18-20, we see that Abraham (Abram at the time) gave tithes to Melchisedec in response to the blessing Abram received from Him. Melchisedec was God's Priest, the minister of the Most High God. It is important to remember that the **first mention of tithes** in the Bible is in the context of the **High Priestly Order of the New Covenant**. Jesus is our High Priest forever after the Order of Melchisedec. It is also important to note that this mention of tithing pre-dates the Law of Moses.

NT Response: The New Testament also teaches gratitude for the ministry received from God's ministers.

> *"Let the elders that rule well be counted worthy of double honour, especially they who labour in the word and doctrine. (18) For the scripture saith, thou shalt not muzzle the ox that treadeth out the corn. And, The labourer is worthy of his reward."*
> (1 Timothy 5:17-18)

Note that Paul quotes from the Law of Moses to validate his teaching of respect and gratitude toward Christian elders, especially those who labor in God's Word and doctrine, and that these ministers are even worthy of double honor.

OT Reason: Appreciation for God, His protection, and provision.

In Genesis 28:15-22, we see Jacob vowing to give God back one-tenth of everything that God gives to him as gratitude for God's protection and provision. Again, we see that Biblical tithing existed before the Law of Moses.

NT Response: The New Testament continues with the concept of giving in response to God's provision and protection.

> *"But this I say, He which soweth sparingly shall reap also sparingly; and he which soweth bountifully shall reap also bountifully. (7) Every man according as he purposeth in his heart, so let him give; not grudgingly, or of necessity: for God loveth a cheerful giver. (8) And **God is able to make all grace abound toward you**; that ye, always having all sufficiency in all things, may abound to every good work:"* (2 Corinthians 9:6-8)

This passage from 2 Corinthians tells us that we can trust in God's provision, allowing us to abound to every good work. It also teaches us to give cheerfully and as we purpose in our heart. However, we cannot ignore verse 6, which tells us if we give sparingly, we will reap only a little, but if we give bountifully, we will reap much.

OT Reason: The tithes of all the land and all the herds are holy unto the Lord. (see Leviticus 27:30-34)

NT Response: Beyond the tithes, everything is God's.

> *"For the earth is the Lord's, and the fulness thereof."* (1 Corinthians 10:26)

OT Reason: Provision for the ministers in the Temple.

Numbers 18:20-32 teaches us that the children of Levi would have no inheritance in the Promised Land. It further states that all the tithe of Israel belonged to the Levites as their reward for their ministry. So, in this case, the tithe was designed to provide for the ministers of God.

NT Response: The concept of providing for those who serve in the Lord's ministry continues in the New Testament.

> *"Do ye not know that they which minister about holy things live of the things of the temple? and they which wait at the altar are partakers with the altar? (14) Even so hath* **the Lord ordained that they which preach the gospel should live of the gospel.***"* (1 Corinthians 9:13-14)

When Paul compares Gospel preachers to the Old Testament priests, he states that Gospel preachers ought to make their living from the Gospel in the same way as the priests of the Temple made their living. How were the priests to earn their living? Primarily from the tithe.

OT Reason: Provision for the stranger, widow, and fatherless.

Deuteronomy 14:22-29 teaches us that the tithe was to be taken up year by year (verse 22). If the distance to God's designated place was too great, it was to be turned into money (verses 24-25). At the appointed time, all the tithe of the increase should be given, so that the Levites, (also strangers, the fatherless, and widows – see below) could have provision.

NT Response: In the previous section, we saw that God continues His provision for His ministers in the New Testament in the same manner as in the Old Testament. It is also clear from the following Scriptures that God intends for His people in the New Testament to care for the widow, the fatherless, and strangers (as appropriate).

*"**Pure religion** and undefiled before God and the Father is this, To **visit the fatherless and widows** in their affliction, and to keep himself unspotted from the world."* (James 1:27)

*"Be not forgetful to **entertain strangers**: for thereby some have entertained angels unawares."* (Hebrews 13:2)

As we can see, God's purpose for New Testament giving also matches that in the Old Testament concerning the fatherless, widows, and strangers.

OT Reason: To Avoid God's Anger and Assure His Blessings.

"Behold, I will send my messenger, and he shall prepare the way before me: and the LORD, whom ye seek, shall suddenly come to his temple, even the messenger of the covenant, whom ye delight in: behold, he shall come, saith the LORD of hosts." (Malachi 3:1)

*"For I am the LORD, I change not; **therefore ye sons of Jacob are not consumed.**"* (Malachi 3:6)

*"Will a man rob God? Yet ye have robbed me. But ye say, Wherein have we robbed thee? In tithes and offerings. (9) **Ye are cursed with a curse:** for ye have robbed me, even this whole nation. (10) Bring ye all the tithes into the storehouse, that there may be meat in mine house, and prove me now herewith, saith the LORD of hosts, if I will not open you the windows of heaven, and pour you out a blessing, that there shall not be room enough to receive it."* (Malachi 3:8-10)

Since Malachi chapter three is often a contentious passage, verses 1 and 6 have been quoted to help establish context.

Verse 1 is a reference to John the Baptist and Jesus. This understanding is widely accepted in conservative Christian circles. Thus verse 1 is prophetic of the forerunner of Jesus the Messiah Himself. Therefore, the context applies to New Testament times and not only to the Jews of Malachi's day.

Verse 6 states that God does NOT change! Just two verses after telling us that God doesn't change, He proceeds to accuse people of robbing God, regarding **tithes and offerings**!

God is angry with His people and pronounces that the whole nation is "… cursed with a curse …"

On the other hand, God pronounces abundant blessings upon them if they will obey God's Word and bring in all the tithes. God is saying that it is not possible for us to out-give Him!

NT Response: The idea of blessings for obedience in giving and curses for disobedience to God's Word is once again clearly evident in the New Testament.

> *"Let him that is taught in the word communicate unto him that teacheth in all good things. (7) **Be not deceived; God is not mocked**: for whatsoever a man soweth, that shall he also reap. (8) For he that **soweth to his flesh shall of the flesh reap corruption**; but he that soweth to the Spirit shall of the Spirit reap life everlasting. (9) And let us not be*

weary in well doing: for in due season we shall reap, if we faint not." (Galatians 6:6-9)

"And another came, saying, Lord, behold, here is thy pound, which I have kept laid up in a napkin: (21) For I feared thee, because thou art an austere man: thou takest up that thou layedst not down, and reapest that thou didst not sow. (22) And he saith unto him, Out of thine own mouth will I judge thee, thou wicked servant. Thou knewest that I was an austere man, taking up that I laid not down, and reaping that I did not sow: (23) Wherefore then gavest not thou my money into the bank, that at my coming I might have required mine own with usury? (24) And he said unto them that stood by, Take from him the pound, and give it to him that hath ten pounds. (25 And they said unto him, Lord, he hath ten pounds.) (26) For I say unto you, That unto every one which hath shall be given; and from him that hath not, even that he hath shall be taken away from him." (Luke 19:20-26)

As is evident, the New Testament associates obedience in stewardship to blessings and cursings. If we sow sparingly, we will reap little. If we do not invest our Lord's talents wisely, the blessings will be taken away from us.

The bottom line is that **God HAS NOT CHANGED!**

Conclusion:

Since the Old Testament reasons for tithing are continued in the New Testament, it is unreasonable to assume that the practice of tithing should not continue as well. New Testament Christians should be able to go far beyond the Old Testament requirements. Why? Because we are empowered by the Holy Spirit to do so! Every New Testament example of Spirit-led giving validates the extravagance of generosity that should be expected from Holy Ghost-enabled believers.

Chapter 26 – Tithing Pre-Dates the Law

Many Christians object to tithing, claiming that we are no longer under the Law. The validity of this claim should be reviewed in light of the Scriptures. In this chapter, we will examine the fact that tithing in the Bible took place prior to God giving the Law to Moses and what impact that might have on this notion.

In hermeneutics (how to accurately interpret and understand the Bible), there exists the "Rule of First Mention." This guideline recommends that one find the first reference in the Bible to a subject or doctrine and study this initial occurrence to gain insight. A review of the onset of a doctrine normally provides insights into the purpose of the doctrine.

By following the "Rule of First Mention" we find out that tithing took place before God gave the Law to Moses. Since God does not change, let's examine these findings.

> *"And Melchizedek king of Salem brought forth bread and wine: and he was the priest of the most high God. And he blessed him, and said, Blessed be Abram of the most high God, possessor of heaven and earth: And blessed be the most high God, which hath delivered thine enemies into thy hand. **And he gave him tithes of all.**"* (Genesis 14:18-20)

The above passage is the first time tithing is mentioned in the Bible; therefore, we need to study it and see what we can learn about this event. In another chapter, we will look at who Melchizedek is, which should add further insight. For now, we will recognize that the Priest of the Most High

God received tithes from Abram, the man of the Most High God. The **purpose** of this tithe was in response to the **blessing** of God through the **servant** of God and **thankfulness** to God for His help in the battle.

It appears to be easy to draw contemporary parallels to this first tithing encounter. Like Abraham, should we not also be **thankful** for the **blessings** we receive from God through His **servants** today? The New Testament says that we should give "...*double honour*..." to our spiritual leaders, those who "...*labour in the word and doctrine*..." (1 Timothy 5:17).

It should also be noted that **Melchizedek is a representative of the New Covenant**, not the Old Covenant. Seven times in the Bible, we are told that **the High Priestly ministry of Jesus was patterned after Melchizedek**. This man is in no way a reflection of the Old Covenant.

In short, Abraham (the father of faith) gave tithes to Melchizedek (after whose New Covenant High Priesthood Jesus' High Priesthood was patterned.) This is a **powerful thought** to ponder.

---

*"And Jacob vowed a vow, saying, If God will be with me, and will keep me in this way that I go, and will give me bread to eat, and raiment to put on, (21) So that I come again to my father's house in peace; then shall the Lord be my God: (22) And this stone, which I have set for a pillar, shall be God's house: and of all that thou shalt give me **I will surely give the tenth unto thee**."*
(Genesis 28:20-22)

Here is another example of tithing pre-dating the Law God gave to Moses. In this case, we see Jacob vowing to give a tenth of all that God gives him as an expression of gratitude for God's provision and protection.

God has not changed. The same God Who provided for Jacob and protected him is our God today. Has anything changed? Should we not also be grateful to God for His kindness to us?

The notion that, because Christians are no longer under the Law, we are not expected to tithe is invalidated by the fact that tithes were given to God before the Law was given. Abraham gave tithes to God's Priest, and Jacob set the example of gratitude to God both before the Law, proving that the concept of tithing did not begin with the Law. These two pre-Law examples demonstrate that it is not a legitimate argument to renounce tithing simply because we are not under the Law. It is meaningful that two of the Old Testament patriarchs voluntarily gave tithes before the Law God gave to Moses.

As is most often the case with the *Rule of First Mention*, subsequent references to the tithe build on the first text. It is evident as one follows the tithe from the Melchizedek priesthood example to the Levitical (or Aaronic) priesthood. The Law of Moses builds upon the priesthood, receiving tithes as an expression of praise and thankfulness to God for His blessings and clarifies additional purposes of the doctrine.

The purposes of tithing are discussed in greater detail in other chapters, especially in Chapter 25. Suffice it to say for this chapter, that the practice of giving tithes to the Priest of God began before the Law.

To briefly summarize this chapter:

* Tithing unto God's Priest (Melchizedek) started before the Law,
* Tithing unto God's ministers continued and was required **by** the Law,
* God **does not change**,
* God still teaches that His servants should make their living from their ministry (1 Corinthians 9:13-14).

The focus of this chapter is to remind the reader that tithing came before God gave the Law to Moses. This fact nullifies the idea that tithing was a result of the Law and thereby no longer applies to Christians under grace.

Chapter 27 – Who Is Melchisedec (aka Melchizedek)?

> *"And blessed be the most high God, which hath delivered thine enemies into thy hand. And he gave him tithes of all."* (Genesis 14:20)

> *"Whither the forerunner is for us entered, even Jesus, made an high priest for ever after the order of Melchisedec."* (Hebrews 6:20)

Considering Melchisedec, we first see that the father of faith, Abraham, gave the first tithes noted in the Bible to Melchisedec. Second, we see that the High Priestly ministry of Jesus Christ is forever patterned after Melchisedec.

It is critically important to understand that the very first tithes in the Bible were given by a highly esteemed man of God (Abraham) to a **New Covenant** priest (Melchisedec). Melchisedec had to be a priest that was reflective of the New Covenant; otherwise, Jesus could not have been patterned after Melchisedec.

The Bible teaches that the Melchisedec order priesthood was superior to the priesthood of the Old Covenant. The Levitical (Old Covenant) priesthood could not bring perfection, but the Melchisedec (New Covenant) priesthood could, and did through Jesus Christ!

> *"If therefore perfection were by the Levitical priesthood, (for under it the people received the law,) what further need was there that another priest should rise after the order of Melchisedec, and not be called after the order of Aaron?"*

(Hebrews 7:11)

Now that we have firmly established that Melchisedec was indeed a New Covenant representative, and the first recipient of tithes in Scripture, we will move on and examine the question, "Who is Melchisedec?"

While Melchisedec is only briefly mentioned in this account, the fact that Abram gave tithes to this King of Salem may be important in our understanding of the doctrine of tithing for Christians today. Answering the question "Who is Melchisedec?" may also be valuable in our study of tithing.

While it is true that much debate has existed throughout the ages as to the identity of Melchisedec, one can certainly read the Bible and decide for themselves. In this chapter, we will briefly review what the Bible says about Melchisedec; we will summarize this review, and we will suggest a conclusion.

Melchisedec is mentioned in the following passages of Scripture:

* Genesis 14:18-20,
* Psalm 110:4,
* Hebrews 5:10-14,
* Hebrews 6:20,
* Hebrews 7:1-28.

What can we learn from these passages about Melchisedec?

In Genesis 14:18-20, we learn the following:

* He was the King of Salem (Jerusalem),
* King of Salem translates to *King of Peace*,

* He blesses Abram with bread and wine,
* He was the Priest of the Most High God,
* He blesses God,
* Abram gives tithes to Him.

From Psalm 110:4, we see the following:

* God swore an unchangeable oath that Jesus would forever be a Priest after the order of Melchisedec.

Hebrews 5:10-14 is a cryptically telling passage. We are told these facts in these verses:

* The author of Hebrews has much to say about Melchisedec and the priesthood after His order,
* The things the writer wants to say are "hard to utter" because his audience is "dull of hearing."

The vast majority of what we know about Melchisedec is found in Hebrews chapter 7, as follows:

* Melchisedec means "King of Righteousness" (vs. 2),
* He had no father, mother or lineage (vs. 3),
* He had no beginning of days nor end of life (vs. 3),
* He was made like the Son of God (vs. 3),
* He abode as a Priest continually (vs. 3),
* He is greater than Abraham (vs. 4-7),
* He is not descended from Levi (vs. 6),
* Melchisedec did not die (vs. 8),
* Levi paid tithes to Him while yet in Abrahams's loins (i.e., not yet conceived, vs. 9-10),
* Perfection came via the Melchisedec priesthood (vs. 11),
* The priesthood and the Law changed (vs. 12),
* Jesus was after the similitude of Melchisedec (vs. 15),
* Made a priest due to the power of an endless life (vs. 16),
* The Law made nothing perfect (vs. 18-19),

* The Melchisedec priesthood brought a better hope, which did make perfection (vs. 19),
* The Melchisedec priesthood is made by an oath, not by commandment as the Levitical was (vs. 20-21),
* Jesus (Priest after the order of Melchisedec), is the better testament (vs. 22),
* The Levitical priesthood had many priests because each one died. The Melchisedec priesthood continues forever (vs. 23-24),
* The Melchisedec order priesthood can "save to the uttermost" (vs. 25) because He lives forever to make intercession,
* The Melchisedec priesthood is holy, harmless, undefiled, separate from sinners, and made higher than the heavens (vs. 26),
* Jesus (Priest forever after the order of Melchisedec) does not need to offer sacrifices continually. He offered Himself once for all (vs. 27),
* The oath of God regarding the Melchisedec priesthood "…maketh the Son…" (vs. 28).

Our study for this book indicates that Melchisedec was a pre-incarnate appearance of Jesus Christ, and Abraham paid tithes to Melchisedec before the Law. Thus, if Jesus received tithes from Abraham, before the Law, it is likely that Jesus will receive tithes from His people today.

If your beliefs do not lead to Melchisedec being Jesus pre-incarnate, that is not a problem. It is indeed inarguable that Melchisedec was a New Covenant priestly representative who received tithes from Abraham.

> *"See how great this man was to whom Abraham the patriarch gave a tenth of the spoils!"*
> (Hebrews 7:4 ESV)

So much more could be said about the relationship between Melchisedec and Jesus that this author has written a book to address these Bible verses in greater detail. For a more in-depth study, look for **Melchisedec – A Character Study** by Robert W. Dallmann.

Chapter 28 – Melchisedec and Aaronic Priesthoods

The purpose of this chapter is to compare these two priesthoods and demonstrate that both received tithes. The Bible mentions a few different priesthoods. As Christians, the Bible refers to us as a "royal priesthood" (see 1 Peter 2:9) and "kings and priests" unto our God (see Revelation 1:6). Jethro, Moses' father-in-law, is identified as the "priest of Midian."

However, there are two priesthoods ordained explicitly by God with specific duties and importance, and each of these priesthoods was recipients of tithes.

The First Ordained Priesthood

The first (and last) of these God-ordained priesthoods is the Melchisedec priesthood. This Priest is first mentioned in Genesis 14:18, where He blesses God and Abram, and He is blessed by Abram. Greater detail about this priesthood and the relationship to Jesus Christ can be found in Hebrews chapter 7.

This author embraces the belief that Melchisedec was a pre-incarnate appearance of Jesus Christ. Review the chapter entitled "Who is Melchisedec" for more details. Minimally, He was the Priest of the Most High God, and Jesus was a Priest forever after the order of Melchisedec. FOREVER, Jesus is Priest after this priestly order.

No matter what one's belief about the identity of Melchisedec, his priestly order is representative of the New Covenant. Jesus is forever a High Priest after the order of

Melchisedec; therefore, this priestly order cannot be Old Covenant.

The Second Ordained Priesthood

The priesthood that we are likely more familiar with is the Aaronic or Levitical priesthood. This ministry was established by God through the Law given to Moses.

These were highly regulated offices, including a single High Priest. God's Law spelled out detailed qualifications for each priestly duty, and strict standards were to be upheld.

Comparisons

Melchisedec Order compared to the Levitical Priesthood

* The Priest of the Most High God (Gen. 14:18)
- - Many priests including one High Priest (Lev. 1:5)

* Jesus is forever a Priest after the order of Melchisedec (Heb. 5:10)
- - Jesus is a greater High Priest than those ordained by the Law (Heb. 7:11 and 9:11)

* Received tithes from Abram, the father of faith (Gen. 14:20)
- - Received tithes from the children of Israel (Num. 18:24)

* Jesus is a Priest after the order of Melchisedec; therefore, the tithes were given to the Lord (Heb. 5:6)
- - The tithes belong to the Lord (Lev. 27:30)

Chapter 29 – Will A Man Rob God?

> *"**Will a man rob God**? Yet ye have robbed me. But ye say, Wherein have we robbed thee? **In tithes and offerings**."* (Malachi 3:8)

Malachi 3:8 is perhaps the most quoted, most well-known Bible verse when it comes to tithing. Advocates of New Covenant tithing will quote this verse to teach principles of blessings as a result of giving. Opponents of this verse will typically refer to the fact that we are not under the Law. (The notion of not being under the Law is dealt with in chapters 26 and 32.)

While this book adheres to the Old and New Testament teaching of sowing and reaping (e.g., see 2 Corinthians 9:6), this chapter is dedicated to reviewing the context of these passages in Malachi. The notion that Christians can sever themselves from these prophetic words because we are not under the Law seems to be misplaced in the light of surrounding verses.

First - Malachi 3:1-5 – John the Baptist and Jesus the Messiah:

> *"Behold, I will send **my messenger, and he shall prepare the way before me**: and **the LORD**, whom ye seek, shall suddenly come to his temple, even the messenger of the covenant, whom ye delight in: behold, **he shall come, saith the LORD of hosts**."* (Malachi 3:1)

The beginning of Malachi chapter 3 gives excellent insights into the context of these passages about tithing. Malachi

3:1 is prophetic of John the Baptist proclaiming and preparing the way for Jesus.

Malachi 3:2-3 speak of the purifying ministry of Jesus: Jesus is going to purify His people so that they may make offerings of righteousness.

In Malachi 3:4, the prophet states that after this purifying, the people shall give pleasant offerings unto the Lord. The prophet indicates that the Messiah will restore the ability to bring good offerings to the Lord as in the former days.

In verse 5, the prophet discusses the Lord's judgment against various forms of wickedness. Sorcerers, false witnesses, oppressors of the fatherless, laborers, and strangers will be dealt with.

Most Christians do NOT reject John the Baptist or Jesus as applying to New Covenant believers.

Second - Malachi 3:6-7 – A transition from the future to the current day:

> *"For **I am the LORD, I change not**; therefore ye sons of Jacob are not consumed."* (Malachi 3:6)

Malachi 3:6 is critical in reading this chapter. The prophet just completes some amazing words telling of the coming of John the Baptist and Jesus, and then he says, "**I AM** the Lord, and **I DO NOT** change!"

Malachi links John the Baptist and Jesus with the children of Israel's current situation, by stating that the Lord does not change. Then the prophet (speaking by the Holy Spirit) immediately addresses the need for God's people to return to Him. In Malachi 3:7, the Lord tells His people to return to Him, and then He would return to them. Verse 7 also tells us that the people asked a question:

"In what way do we need to return?"

Third - Malachi 3:8 – God answers their question:

> *"Will a man rob God? Yet ye have robbed me. But ye say, Wherein have we robbed thee? In tithes and offerings."* (Malachi 3:8)

Monetary infidelity! God's people were unfaithful in their finances! One would be hard-pressed to make the case that financial infidelity is not a problem in contemporary Christianity.

Remember, this is connected to the prophetic context of the coming of John the Baptist and Jesus the Messiah. God has not changed! Tithing is still exemplary of faithfulness in finances. This principle can be seen throughout the entire Bible. Here are some New Testament examples:

> *"His lord said unto him, Well done, thou good and faithful servant: thou hast been faithful over a few things, I will make thee ruler over many things: enter thou into the joy of thy lord."*
> (Matthew 25:21)

If a person cannot be faithful with a little (the tithe, 10%), how is it possible for God to entrust him with much? This story from Matthew 25 says that even the little that he has will be taken away from him.

> *"And Jesus answering said unto them, Render to Caesar the things that are Caesar's, and to God the things that are God's. And they marvelled at him."*

(Mark 12:17)

In the above passage, Jesus was asked if they should pay taxes to the Romans. Jesus provided an excellent answer. However, there is a question that Christians should ask themselves. "What things belong to God?" The answer is EVERYTHING!

Again, we are left with the question, "If everything belongs to God, and we are not even able to be faithful to give 10% to Him, how can we give Him everything?"

Should we be surprised by the fact that **MONEY** (in the form of tithing discussions) continues to cause significant problems in the church today? The love of money has been and is still the root of all sorts of evil. Perhaps the love of money on the part of believers is the reason that legitimate, God-ordained ministries often lack basic needs.

Fourth - Malachi 3:9 – God pronounces a curse upon the people for robbing Him:

> *"Ye are cursed with a curse: for ye have robbed me, **even this whole nation.**"* (Malachi 3:9)

There are some things to note about this passage. Some opponents of tithing will state that this chapter of Malachi is an indictment against the priests for their abuses. However, verse 9 includes the whole nation in this curse.

Others will attempt to associate this curse with the curse of the Law, and it is an invalid correlation. If we are under the curse of the Law, we are hell-bound. This curse is not dealing with heaven or hell, which is settled by the death, burial, and resurrection of Jesus, the prophesied Messiah.

116

This curse is one associated with the removal of blessings due to robbing God. Is this substantiated in the New Testament? Yes! Here are a few passages for our review.

> *"But this I say, He which soweth sparingly shall reap also sparingly; and he which soweth bountifully shall reap also bountifully."*
> (2 Corinthians 9:6)

While this passage does not state that blessings will be removed, it does indicate that our blessings will be reaped based upon our sowing. Of course, this makes perfect sense. If we sow one fruit seed, we might get one plant. If we sow thousands of seeds, we will get many plants.

> *"Take therefore the talent from him, and give it unto him which hath ten talents. (29) For unto every one that hath shall be given, and he shall have abundance: but from him that hath not shall be taken away even that which he hath. (30) And cast ye the unprofitable servant into outer darkness: there shall be weeping and gnashing of teeth."*
> (Matthew 25:28-30)

In this parable, Jesus teaches that the unfaithful steward would have his talent taken away and be punished. Instead of being faithful, he hid his talent and returned it to the Master with no interest or increase upon His return. This parable ends and Jesus then teaches that the Son of Man would separate the sheep from the goats upon His return.

God desires faithfulness and good stewardship in all areas of our lives. In this case, Jesus used money to teach this truth.

Fifth - Malachi 3:10-12 - God describes His blessing and protection over those who will be faithful:

In verse 10, God tells us to put Him to the test. He says to prove Him and see if He will not open the windows of heaven and pour blessings out on us.

Verse 11 teaches that not only will God bless us, but He will also prevent the enemy from destroying our blessings. The fruit of our labors will be blessed and not devastated.

Lastly, verse 12 tells us that the nations of the world will recognize that God's people are blessed by His hand. God's faithfulness is routinely recognized in the lives of His faithful people. Those who sincerely attempt to live life His way are often perceived as blessed by the world.

Does this blessing of God regarding monetary faithfulness reveal itself in the New Testament? Of course! God does not change! For one example, see 2 Corinthians 9:6 again.

Sixth - Malachi 3:13-15 - The prophet describes the people's bad attitude towards serving God:

These verses state that God's people had come to believe that it was worthless, serving God. They believed that the proud, wicked, and tempters of God were better off than those who feared, loved, and served Him.

The concepts expressed in this passage are not foreign to the New Testament. Review the following Scriptures, and you will see the common thread.

> *"Nay but, O man, who art thou that repliest against God? Shall the thing formed say to him that formed it, Why hast thou made me thus?"* (Romans 9:20)

118

We must keep in mind that all of this continues in the context of incredible Messianic prophecies. God has not changed, and neither have His principles of giving, including the tithing principle.

Seventh - Malachi 3:16-18 - God remembers:

> *"Then they that **feared the LORD spake often one to another**: and the LORD hearkened, and heard it, and a book of remembrance was written before him for them that feared the LORD, and that thought upon his name."* (Malachi 3:16)

In the context of robbing God, the prophet tells us that a *book of remembrance* was written before the Lord: God remembers those who FEAR Him and SPEAK OFTEN of Him.

Amazing! A lack of tithing is associated with a lack of the fear of the Lord, as well as a lack of interest in the things of God (i.e., they don't often speak of God!)

Remember, this is all in the context of prophecies about John the Baptist and Jesus. It is in the context of the Lord never changes. It is in the context of tithing. It seems that monetary fidelity is critically important in the Kingdom of God!

In Malachi 3:17, God tells us that those entered into His *book of remembrance* will be His. He says that He will spare them as a man spares his son that serves Him. Those who fear the Lord and speak of Him often, those who return unto God and are faithful, will be God's, and He will protect them!

Lastly, in verse 18, Malachi prophesies that those who belong to God will discern the righteous and the wicked. That is, they will be able to differentiate those who serve God from those who do not. Suffice it to say; it is an excellent thing to fear God and love Him enough to speak of Him often.

Keep in mind that a lack of faithfulness in tithing is defined by God to be robbing Him. Surely, it is an extreme lack of wisdom to rob from God!

Those who oppose the principle of tithing are guilty of picking and choosing what parts of the Bible they want to accept and what parts they reject. Malachi chapter three is a prime example of this. No true Christian rejects Jesus and His ministry, which is prophesied in this chapter. However, most tithing opponents summarily reject Malachi 3:8-10.

If one is going to reject the verses relevant to tithing in this chapter, to maintain the integrity of interpretation, they must also reject the prophetic words concerning the coming of Jesus. Is any true Christian willing to reject prophecies about Jesus? On what hermeneutical grounds can one reject the middle few verses of this chapter and not the rest?

Chapter 30 – Honor God With Your Giving

*"Honour the Lord with thy **substance**, and with the **firstfruits** of all thine **increase**: (10) So shall thy barns be filled with plenty, and thy presses shall burst out with new wine."* (Proverbs 3:9-10)

In Proverbs 3:9, we see encouragement to honor God with what we already have and with the very best of what we will receive! Godly giving is GENEROUS and from the heart.

Amongst those who oppose the principle of tithing, one of their arguments is that God only required tithes in the form of food (crops) and only from certain people (farmers). This passage demonstrates that Old Covenant adherents did not validate these limitations. Those who desire to limit tithes to crops are true legalists. They cling to a few favored passages (out of context) to reject tithing.

There are a few words from this passage that we need to define, for clarity. With each of these words, we see that there is no farming limitation stated or implied.

Substance = Strong's H1952 – "hown - wealth, riches, substance - price, high value."

By definition, our substance is our existing wealth. As for limiting our tithing (and all our giving) to crops, this Proverb makes it clear that we should honor the Lord with all we hold dear, everything we possess and value!

Firstfruits = Strong's H7225 – "re'shiyth - first, beginning, best, chief - choice part."

Again, we see that there is no limitation to farming in this word. We are encouraged to honor God with the first and best of what He has given us.

Increase = Strong's H8393 – "tĕbuw'ah - produce, product, revenue - income – gain."

While substance speaks to that which we already possess, this word applies to future wealth, our income or revenues. This Proverb is telling us that honoring God with the best of our wealth and our income is the right thing to do.

Lastly, we can see the truth of Malachi 3:6 where God tells us that He does not change, when we compare the above passage with 2 Corinthians 9:6-7 below.

> *"But this I say, He which **soweth sparingly shall reap also sparingly**; and he which **soweth bountifully shall reap also bountifully**. (7) Every man according as he purposeth in his heart, so let him give; not grudgingly, or of necessity: for God loveth a cheerful giver."* (2 Corinthians 9:6-7)

In both covenants, we see that honoring God with our giving leads to His blessings! It is truly wonderful to serve an unchanging God!

Chapter 31 – Test God

*"Bring the full tithe into the storehouse, that there may be food in my house. **And thereby put me to the test**, says the Lord of hosts, if I will not open the windows of heaven for you and pour down for you a blessing until there is no more need... Then all nations will call you blessed, for you will be a land of delight, says the Lord of hosts."*
(Malachi 3:10, 12 ESV)

Put God to the test???

In researching this topic, no other Scripture could be found whereby God challenges His people to TEST HIM! When one ponders this thought, it is truly awe-inspiring!

About the possessions He entrusts to our stewardship, God challenges people to put Him to the test! Is it possible that God is going to fail the test? **NO!**

So, what does God mean when He tells us to **"test"** Him concerning our finances?

Some teach this as a formula to force God to give them money. That is a faulty application of this passage based on partial truths from the Bible.

Indeed, it is true that this passage teaches God will pour out His blessings in response to this test. However, the context refers to a corporate/national setting, which is evident in the context of the passage.

In context, it is inappropriate to attempt to manipulate God into giving you money. However, it is entirely proper to believe that God will surely bless faithfulness in cheerful, generous giving.

When God says, **"test Me,"** precisely what is He challenging His people to do? To answer this, we will look at the definition of the original Greek word for *test* in this passage.

Test = Strong's H974 – "bachan - to examine, try, prove - to examine, scrutinize - to test, prove, try (of gold, persons, the heart, man of God) - to be tried, proved - to make a trial."

God is essentially saying, "Be faithful in your tithes and offerings and try me! See if I will not bless you, abundantly! I will!"

Chapter 32 – We Are Not Under the Law!

*"But we know that **the law is good**..."*
(1 Timothy 1:8)

*"For we know that **the law is spiritual**..."*
(Romans 7:14)

*"Wherefore **the law is holy**, and the commandment holy, **and just, and good**."* (Romans 7:12)

Given God's Word, as shown in the New Testament above, what does it mean when believers say, "We are not under the Law. We are under grace."?

Are they saying Jesus died so that we can break or disregard the Law?

The words "we are not under the Law" seem to be the battle cry of Christians who rebel against some notion of obedience. Yet the idea of not being under the Law readily lends itself to the legitimate question, "Are we now allowed to sin?"

> *"What then? shall we sin, because we are not under the law, but under grace? **God forbid**."*
> (Romans 6:15)

Grace does NOT make allowance for sin. Now we need a working definition of "sin." What does the Bible tell us sin is, and how does that impact our obedience to the Law?

> *"...for **sin is the transgression of the law**."*
> (1 John 3:4)

This truth should begin to shed new light upon being under grace. Grace does not allow the recipients of God's grace to sin, and sin is the violation of the Law.

Here is another verse that clarifies God's perspective on the Law:

> *"Do we then make void the law through faith?* **God forbid***: yea, we establish the law."* (Romans 3:31)

So what does it mean when the Bible says we are not under the Law?

> *"But if ye be led of the Spirit, ye are not under the law."* (Galatians 5:18)

> *"For sin shall not have dominion over you: for ye are not under the law, but under grace."* (Romans 6:14)

> *"For Christ is the end of the law for righteousness to every one that believeth."* (Romans 10:4)

The bottom line to not being under the Law is in the light of salvation. Jesus is the end of the Law for RIGHTEOUSNESS!

Notice that **Jesus is not the end of the Law**, but rather the **end of the Law as it pertains to righteousness**. The Law is part of God's Word, and God says that His Word will never pass away (see Matthew 24:35).

God expects us to keep the Law that pertains to moral issues. It is only a problem to those who attempt to earn salvation by keeping His Law.

God expects you to keep His Moral Law:

* God **EXPECTS** us to love Him with all our heart, strength, soul, and mind,

* God **EXPECTS** us to not murder,

* God **EXPECTS** us not to lie,

* God **EXPECTS** us not to covet our neighbor's spouse (or property),

* God **EXPECTS** us not to steal.

What aspects of the Law does God expect us to keep, and how does the tithe fit into that?

> *"For verily I say unto you, **Till heaven and earth pass**, one jot or one tittle shall in no wise pass from the law, **till all be fulfilled**."* (Matthew 5:18)

First, according to Jesus, none of the Law has passed away, since Heaven and earth are still here. This fact immediately gives rise to many legitimate questions.

If the Law is not yet done away with, why don't we still sacrifice animals? Why don't we still stone people? Etc.

The answer to these questions lies in studying which parts of the Law have been completely fulfilled and which sections are still being fulfilled today, as follows:

SACRIFICIAL LAWS - These have been completely fulfilled in Jesus! We should never make sacrifices for sins again since the Lamb of God, Jesus Christ, died once for all, and His sacrifice is eternally perfect!

> *"But this man, after **he had offered one sacrifice for sins for ever**, sat down on the right hand of God;"* (Hebrews 10:12)

PENAL LAWS - These have also been completely fulfilled in Jesus. Jesus paid the price, the penalty, for sin. Therefore, we must no longer exact the penalties for sin required in the penal laws.

> *"For **ye are bought with a price**: therefore glorify God in your body, and in your spirit, which are God's."* (1 Corinthians 6:20)

TEMPLE / CEREMONIAL LAWS - Since the Temple no longer exists and has been replaced by the Body of Christ, the physical applications of these laws are no longer a mandate for the Temple building. There may, of course, be spiritual applications.

> *"What? know ye not that **your body is the temple** of the Holy Ghost which is in you, which ye have of God, and ye are not your own?"*
> (1 Corinthians 6:19)

MORAL LAWS - Jesus obeyed them all. These are the laws God also expects us to follow. God still expects us not to steal, murder, covet, etc. It is these laws that we should fulfill every day through love, following the example of Jesus.

> *.."..therefore **love is the fulfilling of the law**."*
> (Romans 13:10)

Since love is the fulfillment of these Moral Laws, how does that look? What is the practical outworking of that?

The law says, "Don't steal." Love says, "I won't steal from you because I love you."

The law says, "Don't covet." Love says, "I won't covet your things because I love you."

The law says, "Tithe." Love says, "I will give generously because I love you, Lord."

This is the practicality of love: Love leads to obedience!

So, what has changed? Motivation and Ability!

How have motivation and ability changed?

Under the Law

* Motivation = earning something from God (salvation, favor, blessings, etc.),

* Ability = self-effort.

Under Grace

* Motivation = love for God and what He has done for us, and others,

* Ability = the indwelling Holy Spirit; it is no longer I but Christ.

> *"For this is the love of God, that we keep his commandments: and his commandments are not grievous."* (1 John 5:3)

"And this is his commandment, That we should believe on the name of his Son Jesus Christ, and love one another, as he gave us commandment." (1 John 3:23)

"This I say then, Walk in the Spirit, and ye shall not fulfil the lust of the flesh." (Galatians 5:16)

Since this is a book about tithing, how does this train of thought apply to giving our tithes?

Review Chapter 25, "**The Purposes Of Tithes.**" *Some* of the reasons for tithing include thanksgiving to God, supporting God's ministers, helping the poor, etc.

All these Biblical purposes for tithes **are based in morality**. It is morally right for believers to be thankful to God. It is a moral issue for Christians to support God's ministers fully and to help the poor.

Tithes, and more accurately, Spirit-led giving are an aspect of the moral law of God. Therefore, it continues to be applicable until the time when all has been fulfilled (i.e., Jesus' return).

Observations:

Most assuredly, we are not under the Law as a means of salvation. No one has ever been saved by obedience to the Law.

We are not expected to keep the sacrificial, penal, or ceremonial aspects of the Law. Those have been completely fulfilled in Jesus.

God does expect us to fulfill love, for "love is the fulfilling of the law." Therefore, the moral aspects of the Law are still being fulfilled by God's people every day, through LOVE!

Chapter 33 – Free-will Giving vs. Spirit-Led Giving

*"Howbeit when he, the Spirit of truth, is come, **he will guide you into all truth**..."* (John 16:13)

*"For as many as are **led by the Spirit of God**, they are the sons of God."* (Romans 8:14)

*"This I say then, **Walk in the Spirit**, and ye shall not fulfil the lust of the flesh."* (Galatians 5:16)

As a follower of Jesus, the Bible repeatedly tells us that we are to be led by the Holy Spirit. We are to walk in the Holy Spirit. The Holy Ghost will lead us into all truth.

With such an emphasis on being led by God's Spirit, is it even conceivable that God would prefer our free-will giving as opposed to Holy Spirit-led giving?

Should we, as Christians, be led by the Holy Spirit concerning our giving? Or, should we trust in our free-will to give in a manner that honors God?

Of course, we should be guided by the Holy Ghost in every aspect of our lives, and this includes our giving!

The difference between *free-will* and *Spirit-led* giving can be stated as follows:

Free-will Giving - You are free to give. You are free not to give.

Spirit-led Giving - You are free to obey. You are free to disobey.

Chapter 34 – Words To The Unbeliever

If you are a person who is not a Christian, yet you have undertaken to read this book, the following is for you.

Spiritual Truth

*"But the natural man receiveth not the things of the Spirit of God: for they are foolishness unto him: **neither can he know them**, because they are spiritually discerned."* (1 Corinthians 2:14)

The Bible tells us that an unbeliever **cannot** understand spiritual things. Spiritual truth must be comprehended spiritually! Therefore, if you do not know Jesus Christ as your personal Savior, having read this book has likely been awkward. You need to be introduced to the Gospel, which will open your heart and mind to spiritual wisdom. So please, **READ ON** as the Gospel is now presented to you.

The Gospel of Jesus Christ

*"Moreover, brethren, **I declare unto you the gospel** which I preached unto you…By which also ye are saved…For I delivered unto you **first of all**…how that **Christ died for our sins** according to the scriptures; And that **he was buried**, and that **he rose again the third day** according to the scriptures: And that he was seen… of above five hundred brethren at once;…"*
(1 Corinthians 15:1-6)

To become a Christian, you must completely entrust yourself to Jesus Christ, for God's Word says:

* No one is in right standing with God. *"...There is none righteous, no, not one:"* (Romans 3:10)

* You must believe that you are a sinner who has earned God's wrath, judgment, and punishment. *"For the wages of sin is death..."* (Romans 6:23)

* You must believe that Jesus Christ died on the cross for you, in your place, and for your sins. *"But God commendeth his love toward us, in that, while we were yet sinners, Christ died for us."* (Romans 5:8)

* You must believe that Jesus was buried and rose from the dead in victory for you. There were more than five hundred (500) eyewitnesses to His resurrection! *"For to this end Christ both died, and rose..."* (Romans 14:9)

If you truly repent and accept Jesus Christ as your Savior and Lord, you will be a Christian. You can pray a prayer like the one below to express your sincere faith toward God.

Dear God,

I know that I am a sinner, and I deserve eternal punishment, which the Bible calls hell. I am sorry for not living my life the way you require.

Thank you for sending Jesus, Your Son, to die on the cross in my place for my sins. Please forgive me, Father. Thank You for Your love and forgiveness.

I give my life to You. I want You to live in me. I ask You to help me live for Your glory.

In Jesus' Name, Amen.

If you have made this sincere commitment to Jesus, you will want to find a Bible-believing, God-honoring, Jesus-loving, Holy Spirit-led church. Spiritual growth and maturity is God's desire for you. This is what the early church did to mature in their faith:

> *"And they continued stedfastly in the **apostles' doctrine** and **fellowship**, and in **breaking of bread**, and in **prayers**."* (Acts 2:42)

Finding a solid church to be a part of will help you in these things.

You can also contact ChristLife, Inc. ministries to obtain teaching materials that can help in your new spiritual life.

ChristLife, Inc.:
PO Box 1033 - Niagara Falls, NY 14304
Phone: 716.622.7320
Email: Christlife@Christ-like.net